# MEN'S FASHION
## IN THE TWENTIETH CENTURY

*From frock coats to intelligent fibres*

Printed in Spain
for the publishers
Costume & Fashion Press
an imprint of
Quite Specific Media Group Ltd.
260 Fifth Avenue, Suite 703
New York, NY 10001

(212) 725-5377 voice, (212) 725-8506 fax
email: info@quitespecificmedia.com

Other Quite Specific Media Group Ltd.
imprints:
Drama Publishers
By Design Press
EntertainmentPro
Jade Rabbit

http://www.quitespecificmedia.com

ISBN 0-89676-225-4

# MEN'S FASHION
## IN THE TWENTIETH CENTURY
*From frock coats to intelligent fibres*

Maria Costantino

**COSTUME & FASHION PRESS**
New York
an imprint of
Quite Specific Media Group Ltd.

# Contents

# Men's Fashion at the Beginning of the Twentieth Century

Men's fashion at the beginning of the twentieth century can be seen as being divided into two camps: at one extreme, the luxury made-to-measure garments for the wealthy; at the other, less expensive, mass-produced ready-to-wear clothes that imitated the styles of the custom-made models. Although it was the quality of the fabrics and the cut that differentiated custom-made from ready-made clothes, it was the rules governing dress – what to wear, when to wear it and, importantly, how it was worn – that would distinguish the wearer as a 'gentleman'.

Despite a growing number of *nouveaux riches* – the descendants of nineteenth-century industrialists, whose profits had been carefully invested and were now to be enjoyed – in Europe society was still dominated by the aristocracy whose ancestral lands brought privilege, prestige and power. Further down the social scale were the middle-class professionals, doctors, lawyers, bankers and stockbrokers, closely followed by the 'small businessmen': shopkeepers and traders. At the bottom were the labouring or working class and the unemployed.

Yet despite the distinct life-styles of these social groups and the hereditary authority in matters of fashion assumed by the upper class, each was to introduce subtle changes to the pattern of men's fashions both at this time and subsequently throughout the century.

The crucial figure in the history of men's fashions in the early years of the century was Edward, Prince of Wales, later King Edward VII, who epitomized male stylishness and whose wardrobe was copied throughout the world. When 'Bertie', as he was known, visited the German spa resort of Marienbad, it was said that tailors from all of Europe followed his every move, making notes and taking photographs of his outfits. But as well as setting the rules that polite society was supposed to follow, Bertie took many liberties in dress – liberties that he would not allow in others. When Lord Rosebery arrived at Windsor Castle in plain clothes instead of 'full-fig' ceremonial uniform, Edward remarked that he presumed Rosebery had come in the entourage of the American ambassador. The

Prince was especially scathing about the American sense of dress, in particular, brightly-coloured ties and ornately-decorated waistcoats. Nevertheless, many Americans had made their way into London society circles. A severe economic depression in the 1870s had affected British agriculture particularly badly and many of the landed aristocracy found their incomes severely curtailed. Numerous penniless lords, dukes, earls and barons rushed across the Atlantic to find themselves American heiress brides. They returned home not only with a wife (and her fortune) but with one of the first American fashion statements of the twentieth century: flat hair. This 'plastered down' style was achieved by soaking the hair and wrapping the head in linen bandages while it dried, and became very much 'in it' — the latest phrase for being up-to-date.

Above: Edward, Prince of Wales (left) and the Royal party on their way to Ascot. In this photograph, Bertie wears a casual light coloured top hat and open frock coat in contrast to the Duke of Cambridge (centre) who retains the more formal black topper.

Left: Silent movie star Rudolph Valentino with the 'flat' hairstyle made popular in America and later in Britain. The look was achieved by soaking the hair and wrapping the head in linen bandages until it dried.

## Frock Coats, Morning Coats and Lounge Suits

Up to the beginning of the twentieth century the black frock coat and the black silk top hat were 'correct' dress for gentlemen for all society events during the daytime. On an 'ordinary' day, say, for instance, at the races, a gentleman might attend in a tweed suit. But if royalty were present, then the sombre black outfit was compulsory.

'Tum-Tum', as the Prince of Wales was known in Europe because of his gargantuan appetite, had a strong dislike of constricting clothes, in particular, the military uniforms of the regiments with which he held rank. As he

Correct dress for gentlemen at all society events – even an Eton v. Harrow school cricket match – consisted of a black frock coat and black silk top hat. The boys are miniature versions of their fathers, but wear their school shirts with an Eton Collar.

grew older, the Prince also became much fatter. In 1895 he asked his tailors to make an 'open' version of the frock coat where the two sides were held together by a chain with a button at each end. As well as being more comfortable than being completely buttoned up in a heavy wool coat, the open frock coat also flattered Tum-Tum's figure, revealing the decorative details on his waistcoat.

Despite this royal re-styling, the frock coat was to go into a decline at the turn of the century and was replaced by the morning coat. Despite retaining an aura of respectability for

the middle classes in Britain – it would remain for some time part of their church-going wardrobe – the frock coat moved from 'ordinary' dress to 'formal' dress.

The morning coat, when worn with black or grey trousers (often striped) was popular precisely because it was semi-formal and could

therefore be worn in the afternoons as well as in the mornings. Nevertheless, by the early years of the first decade of the new century, the most common town suit was the lounge suit. The forerunner of today's business suit, the jacket fell straight (that is, it was not fitted at the waist) and was wide at the shoulders with small

In this photograph (1913), Rupert Brooke and Duncan Campbell wear lounge suits, the most common town suit at this time. The jacket fell straight, was wide at the shoulders but had small lapels and fastened high at the front. Note the trouser turn-ups , a fashion innovation credited to the Prince of Wales.

Gentlemen's clothing illustrations from Grafton Fashions for 1924-1925. The figure on the left models a Chesterfield, a single-breasted, fly-fronted wool coat with a velvet collar. The bowler-hatted gentleman on the right is wearing a lounge suit, the forerunner of the modern business suit. Apart from details like the spats, lapel shape and trouser length, the London 'City Gentleman's' outfit remained standard until the late 1960s.

lapels and four buttons that fastened high up the front.

It was usually worn with narrow trousers and by 1910 became the 'uniform' of urban middle and lower classes. In theory, aristocracy and 'society' would only have worn lounge suits for the most casual occasions, but the Prince of Wales upset the established system by arriving at Goodwood races in a lounge suit and Homburg hat when everyone else was 'correctly' attired in formal black morning suits.

For outerwear, the Chesterfield was considered to be the most elegant of town overcoats. This was a single-breasted, fly-fronted coat with a velvet collar. In both town and country an Ulster, a loose-fitting, calf-

length, double-buttoning tweed coat with either a half or a full belt, or a MacFarlane, a cape-style coat of the sort that Sherlock Holmes would have worn, were both stylish and practical. By the early twentieth century the mackintosh had developed from its original head-to-toe rubber-smelling 'tent', designed to keep the wearer completely shielded from the elements, into the raincoat to be manufactured by companies like Aquascutum and Thomas Burberry. The latter's 'Walking Burberry', a straight-cut smock-like raincoat with fly-front fastening and raglan sleeves, was one of the most popular styles in the early years of this century.

## Evening Elegance

The arrival of the lounge suit was to have many effects on men's fashions. Tailors were judged on their skills in measuring, cutting and making up such outfits, and the short jacket of the lounge suit was also to influence evening clothes with the introduction of the dinner jacket.

The exact origin of the dinner jacket is unclear. The English claim its descent from the smoking jackets worn by gentlemen after dinner when they retired to the billiards room for brandy and cigars. In order not to offend the ladies with the odours of tobacco smoke when they re-joined them, heavy brocade or quilted jackets were placed over their clothes to protect them from the fumes. In America, the Tuxedo is reputed to have been born at the Tuxedo Park Club in 1886 when the stylish Griswold Lorillard turned up wearing one. This scandalous informal dress attracted a great deal of attention and, subsequently, many followers. Meanwhile, the French claim the jacket as their own 'Monte Carlo', originating on the Riviera where its lightweight qualities were much appreciated by casino goers on summer evenings. Whatever its origins, the dinner jacket was at first considered casualwear. Only later in the early twentieth century did it assume an air of formality. Always black – although the Prince of Wales did have one in midnight blue – dinner jackets were properly worn at informal family dinners, at intimate parties and at the theatre.

For many, however, the true evening suit remained a black tail coat, a black or white waistcoat, white shirt and white tie – black ties could only be worn with dinner jackets – black trousers and black patent leather shoes. While in the first decade of the century the dinner jacket did not completely replace the tail

The dinner jacket or tuxedo (left) gradually made in-roads as eveningwear. Always black, it was only properly worn at informal, family dinners, intimate parties or sometimes to the theatre. Evening dress (right) for most men at this time meant a black tail coat, black trousers, a black or white waist-coat, white shirt and white tie.

coat, the latter would increasingly become restricted to only the most formal occasions.

Once again the Prince of Wales was to make his mark on men's fashions. Edward decided to alter the evening suit by lowering the height of the waistcoat to reveal more shirt front. Despite the fact that this made the starched fronts of dinner shirts more prone to food stains, the lowered neckline of the waistcoat was no doubt less constricting for the Prince, who, legend has it, when feeling bloated during a meal also undid the bottom button of his waistcoat. While these buttons had been left undone in the nineteenth century, the Prince's gesture sanctioned the detail as a fashion statement and the subsequent interest in waistcoats would ensure their place in men's fashions, either as part of the three-piece suit or worn without a jacket both as informal eveningwear and leisurewear from the 1960s onwards.

## Practical Elegance

In spite of the increasingly imposing stature of the Prince of Wales, the early years of the century saw men take an increased interest in sports and physical exercise as well as more sedate activities such as country walks, sea bathing and spa vacations. Although not an outstanding sportsman, the Prince nevertheless demonstrated an interest in this lifestyle with a wardrobe that promoted practicality coupled with a understated elegance. Consequently, he was credited with further major fashion innovations: the introduction of the Norfolk jacket and the wearing of trousers with a crease and cuffs or turn-ups.

At Sandringham, the royal estate in Norfolk, Edward decreed that it was not necessary for either him or his guests to change their clothes the usual four times a day – morning suit,

The Prince of Wales actively promoted a male wardrobe that was elegant yet practical. The Norfolk suit was soon adopted by high society as a shooting outfit.

hunting clothes, back into morning suit during the afternoon and then evening dress for dinner. Twice would suffice: shooting tweeds during the day and evening dress for dinner were now the only outfits required. But, finding most jackets very restricting, the Prince asked his tailors to devise a fuller jacket that would allow him to swing his gun more easily. The tweed Norfolk jacket – belted and with two vertical box pleats at the front and back – allowed for greater movement. At first the Norfolk jacket was worn with knickerbockers which did not match the jacket. Later, however, matching knickerbockers completed the Norfolk suit which soon became adopted by society for shooting parties and by the more affluent middle classes as 'weekend in the country' wear. The Norfolk jacket – even if the knickerbockers are no longer considered fashionable – remains the archetypal country gentleman's jacket.

Trouser cuffs, both a practical and stylish innovation, date from the late nineteenth century when flannel-clad sportsmen would roll their trousers up by hand in an effort to protect them from soiling and to aid mobility. The Prince of Wales was, once again, the sartorial hero when he arrived in the muddy paddock at Ascot races with his trousers turned-up to stop them getting wet. Despite the practical nature of this style detail, it met with some resistance. In 1893 Viscount Lewisham outraged the British Parliament when he wore turned up trousers, and French gentlemen were required to turn down their cuffs before they entered their clubs. By 1900, however, turn-ups were widespread and could be seen in men's fashion catalogues throughout Europe. On the streets they were largely restricted to lounge suits and were worn straight and high, but in subsequent years tailors the world over would argue over their correct height and angle of cut – whether cuffed trousers should break straight across the top of the shoe or be

Above: The future Edward VIII was a fashion trend-setter equal to his grandfather and an ambassador for fashion and fabrics. On his overseas visits – such as here in Canada in 1919 – the Prince was followed closely by photographers and journalists who reported on his wardrobe.

Right: First worn by rowing crews in the 1870s, the straw boater became synonymous with summer. By the twentieth century, boaters were being worn in the city by both young men and women and, when teamed with a striped blazer and flannels, it completed the 'sporting look'.

cut lower to drop over the heel.

A further legend involving the Prince of Wales has him being caught in a sudden rain shower. He gave his soaked trousers to a village tailor for drying and pressing and, when they were returned, found that a crease had been pressed into both legs. What the story doesn't tell us is whether the crease was at the sides of the legs or down the front. Creases at the sides came from the practice of folding trousers flat when they were put away. Front creases appeared in the last years of the nineteenth century but only from the knee down. By 1900 the long, straight, waist-high creases at the front made available by the arrival of the

specially-designed trouser press had become popular. When the Prince adopted the style of the long front crease it finally became associated with stylishness and has remained so throughout the century.

## A Head for Fashion

Very few men at the beginning of this century dared go hatless. Synonymous with the most elegant dressers was the top hat. Daywear in the nineteenth century, by 1900 the topper was increasingly reserved for eveningwear or the most formal occasions. Top hats were

fragile, expensive and difficult to maintain – they required brushing with a specially made velvet pad to raise the sheen and were kept safely in sturdy shaped leather cases – and many of the rituals of top hat etiquette also began to be forgotten. A gentleman tipped his hat when entering a public place only if there were ladies present, and when visiting he would hold his hat in his hand – never setting it down – and in such a way that only the outside and never the lining was visible. In the twentieth century the topper was to be replaced as daytime wear by the bowler or derby. Although the British call this hat after the firm that manufactured them, at Lockes, the hatters in St James, London, it is still referred to as a 'Coke' after William Coke who first commissioned the hat from them. In America, the brown 'derby' was popularized by public figures like New York governor Al Smith but with the origin and name of the hat credited to Edward Stanley, 2nd Earl of Derby, who instituted the famous Derby horse race held in June each year at Epsom. This hard crowned hat does indeed bear a passing resemblance to a jockey's cap. Whatever we choose to call it, this hat was the one that become identified particularly with the 'City Gents' up until the 1970s.

Other fashionable hats at the beginning of this century include the Homburg, the Panama and the boater. The Homburg, made of stiff felt with a centre crease and roll brim, became increasingly worn after the Prince of Wales was presented with one following a visit to Homburg in Germany. Up to that time it had only been worn as a 'country' hat but Bertie wore his to the races in 1889 and the Homburg grew in popularity. By the 1930s black versions became stylish 'town' hats, largely due to the example of Anthony Eden, the head of the British Foreign Office. The Panama, a light-coloured, tightly woven straw

Far left: Two gentlemen take the air in Monte Carlo. The older man on the left wears a bowler or derby and spats or gaiters over his shoes. His younger companion is more casually dressed in straw boater, soft collared shirt and the rounded-toe American 'walking' shoe.

Left: The Panama. This tightly woven, light coloured straw hat in fact originally came from Equador and during the 1850s in France was considered a luxurious summer season dress hat. In 1906 it became known as a Panama when President Roosevelt wore one during a tour of the Panama Canal.

Sir Anthony Eden, Head of the British Foreign Office, seen in 1935 wearing a Homburg, a stiff felt hat with a centre crease and roll brim.

hat, in fact comes from Ecuador and was first worn in high society by Napoleon III who had seen it exhibited at the Exposition Universelle in Paris in 1855. Initially a luxurious dress hat worn during the summer season, it was not until 1906 that it became called a 'Panama' when President Theodore Roosevelt wore one during a tour of the Panama Canal, thereby setting a trend among American men. First worn by rowers in the 1870s, the boater is synonymous with summer and the casual style of dress that can be seen in the paintings of the French Impressionists. By the turn of the century boaters were also clearly visible on city streets on the heads of young men and young women. For men, a boater teamed with a striped blazer and flannel trousers became part of the sporting look of the 1910s and 1920s, a look that would in the 1980s be revived in the film *Chariots of Fire* (1981) and the television series *Brideshead Revisited* (1981).

Sir Tom Talbot Leyland in 1914. On the eve of World War I top hats were only worn in the evenings or for the most formal occasions. Its increased popularity was aided by improved availability in both specialist men's outfitters and in the new department stores.

# A Stiff Upper Lip

Despite the pattern of dress set by the aristocracy in the early years of the twentieth century and the activities of the few remaining dandies and aesthetes, most men in matters sartorial found themselves restricted by financial and practical circumstances.

By 1910, the epitomes of the 'leisure and pleasure'-seeking gentleman – Oscar Wilde, the Prince de Sagan and Jean Lorain, the drug-addicted sado-masochist on whom Marcel Proust had based the character of Baron Charlus – were all dead. So too was fun-loving Bertie, Edward VII. Those who had survived, like Boniface, Marquis de Castellane-Novejean, soon lost their aura of credibility and were replaced by 'new men' who deliberately distanced themselves from 'idle rich' codes of dress and behaviour, dressing instead to confirm their role in a new male order – a mechanized and industrial order.

As Edward VII had rebelled against his militaristic upbringing by his parents Queen Victoria and Prince Albert, so, too, was Edward's son and heir to react against the liberal attitudes of the late monarch. George V was a traditionalist not a trendsetter. Moreover, with a career in the Royal Navy, George was disciplined and prompt and expected all rules, including those regarding dress, to be strictly observed. Norfolk suits were fine for the country, as were bowler hats, but for town George insisted on 'correct dress' and attempted to put back the clock by wearing the black frock coat long after it had become unfashionable.

## Taking Care of Business

The workplace required a suitably serious outlook and an appearance in which masculinity was dominant. The lounge suit lost its former associations with leisure and, because of its practical and multi-purpose nature, became the basis of the modern business suit and the wardrobe for white collar workers worldwide. Available in a limited range of dark, muted colours, the business suit became the multi-

## The Rise of Ready-to-Wear

occasion garment whose plainness was to be relieved only by the choice of tie, the selection of which was governed by discretion. Any 'peacocky' ornamentation was viewed with suspicion as a possible threat to masculine values. Such values were articulated at the time by many fathers including President Roosevelt, whose favourite expression was 'Don't flinch, don't fail, hit the line hard.' It was the age of the 'stiff upper lip' and 'doing the right thing': attitudes that were to be shattered in the trenches of Flanders and France during the First World War.

The adoption of the business suit as the basis of the modern man's wardrobe was aided by the increase in availability of ready-to-wear clothing, both in specialist shops – men's outfitters such as those found on London's Jermyn Street off Piccadilly – and in the department stores, which at this time were at their zenith. In America, a few of the best-known men's outfitters had actually opened in the early 1800s. Henry Brooks began his clothiers business in 1818 and since 1850 has been famous as Brooks Brothers.

George V, the Duke of York and Prince George at the wedding of Princess Maud of Fife. George V is dressed the most formally of the three in a frock coat.

In 1826 Samuel Lord and George Washington Taylor joined forces to open the first Lord and Taylor store in New York while Jordan Marsh and Company in Boston maintained that they could create an outfit from start to finish in half a day. Still prospering after more than a century are John Wannamaker in Philadelphia – the first department store lit by electricity and, in 1900, the first to install a private branch exchange of the Bell telephone system – Joseph Hudson in Detroit, Morris Rich in Atlanta, B. Altman, Adam Gimbel and of course R.H. Macy, whose Herald Square branch is the largest department store in the country.

In Britain in 1909 the American Gordon Selfridge opened his magnificent new store on Oxford Street with an army trumpeter blowing a fanfare from the parapet over the main doors. Selfridges joined Debenham and Freebody, Jays, Marshall and Snelgrove and John Lewis to create London's premier shopping street.

In the traditional tailoring trade each garment was made separately by a single worker, a practice known as the 'complete garment system' that continues today in the bespoke tailors of London's Savile Row. In medieval Europe, tailors had been among the first independent craftsmen and had set up their own guilds and associations. Travelling tailors also called at villages and farms, making clothes for entire households before moving on to the next village. Although the trade of travelling tailors died out in the nineteenth century, in contemporary menswear manufacturing the concept has recently been revived. Largely because they only require transport, a mobile phone and a ready army of outworkers to make up the suits (rather than the expenses incurred by a tailor who rents a shop, keeps a full-time staff and has to invest in stock), the travelling tailors of today claim to offer a bespoke service at less than half the price of a custom-made suit.

In both Britain and America it was at the end of the nineteenth century that the mass-produced clothing industry took off. The major technological advances in clothing manufacture brought about by the introduction of the sewing machine and fabric cutting machinery made it possible to mass produce credible copies of garments that previously, because of the skills required and the cost of labour, could only be produced in tailors' workshops. The advent of clothing factories created a deep division between long-established craftsmen-tailors and the new

Many men who could afford the service continued to have their suits tailored, or 'made-to-measure'. In traditional tailoring, each garment is made separately by a single worker, a practice known as the 'complete garment system'.

casual and semi-skilled workers whose ranks were swollen in the early years of the twentieth century by large numbers of women and immigrant workers, in particular, Jewish refugees in flight from pogroms in Russia and Poland. In many instances these refugees were already skilled tailors: barred from many trades and professions in their countries of origin, this was one of the few areas left open to them. From among the Jewish immigrants to both Britain and America were to come many of the innovators in the clothing manufacture and retailing industries.

## The New Man's Profile

The serious character of the business suit –
and the man who wore it – was to be
challenged by the young and the avant-garde.
Young men no longer wanted to look like
their autocratic fathers, whose dress and
outlook belonged to the Victorian age, and
so they devised for themselves a completely
new and essentially modern image.

In this decade marked by a general
'speeding up' of life – the 1910s marked the
beginning of our infatuation with the
automobile, air travel and global
communications – the male silhouette entered
a new phase. Gone was the waistless 'sack suit'
of 1900 with its short tails, small lapels and
four high buttons that when closed offered a
small glimpse of a torturously starched, or
even stiff cellulose, collar.

In its place was a single-breasted jacket
with two or three closely spaced buttons, a
high, slightly nipped in waist and naturally
sloping shoulders, which was worn with
narrow, cuffed trousers cut short above the
ankle to reveal boots or shoes in the popular
'American style'. By 1910 this style was so
ubiquitous that many mass manufacturers
produced no other. These shoes had a more
rounded (and comfortable) toe than their
European counterparts. Where the French and
English shoes were narrower and suited to
riding, the American shoe with its broguing (a
decorative pattern of punched holes) and soles
that extended beyond their vamps were more
suited to walking. In addition the American
shoe featured a raised heel and wide laces that
the more foppish would tie in a large bow.

Whiskers were banished with a few strokes
of the new, easy-to-use Gillette safety razors.
Gone too was a preference for a heavy-set body:
the new generation undertook rigorous exercise
through boxing, gymnastics and swimming to
provide a slim, youthful body shape.

Above: The latest men's fashion in
lounge suits available at John
Barker's department store,
Kensington, London in 1924.

Right: Men's shoes in a variety of
styles and patterns – perfect for
'cutting a rug' in the 'Roaring
Twenties' – on display at the
International Shoe and Leather
Fair held at the Royal Agricultural
Hall in London, October 1925.

Far right: Dancing the tango at
Brighton Beach, New York in 1914.
Like women bathers, men were
required – by law – to cover upon
public beaches. It was not until
the 1930s that some men on private beaches did away with their
swimming shirts.

Standard dress for male tennis players – professional and amateur – until the mid 1930s was a white, long-sleeved shirt and long, white flannel trousers (which could be rolled up to the ankle). Not until 1932, when U.S. Champion Bunny Austin wore shorts at the Men's National Championships at Forest Hills in New York in 1932, were they worn by professional players for competitions, although many had been wearing them for practice.

## Dress Reform and Utopian Dress

The struggle between youth and age was not the only battle that used clothing as its weapon. Waging a war on men's clothing were the 'Hygienic Dress' reformers on the one hand and the advocates of Utopian dress on the other.

From the 1850s onward many artists and

Artist and member of the
Bloomsbury Set Roger Fry wearing
the 'soft clothes' soon to be
championed by Edward VIII.

intellectuals had debated the issue of dress reform for both women and men. The Pre-Raphaelite painters advocated loosely-fitting medieval-style tunics for men while, in 1881, the Rational Dress Society was founded and campaigned against fashions which deformed the body, impeded movement or injured the wearer's health in any way. In their eyes, fashion was positively dangerous. A leading critic of modern male dress was Dr Gustav Jaeger from Stuttgart, who founded his Sanitary Woollen System in 1878. Jaeger was particularly critical of men's trousers, claiming that these 'tubes' of cloth sucked in drafts of air leaving the legs cold and the waist hot, thereby hindering the proper circulation of blood throughout the body. The doctor advised an immediate return to knee-length wool breeches and woollen stockings. In fact all clothes, including underwear, were to be made solely out of pure, undyed virgin wool. Jaeger believed that wool was the only fabric that kept the body warm and allowed for the

Dress reformer in the Strand, London in 1930. Dress reformers disapproved of long trousers, ties, and restrictive garments, favouring shorts and open necked shirts.

Jaeger's 'Sanitary Woollen System' (1878) insisted that all clothing should be made out of wool, the only fabric the Doctor believed kept the body warm and allowed for the evaporation of perspiration. While not scientifically accurate, Jaeger's views were taken seriously enough to warrant the opening of the Jaeger shop on London's Regent Street.

Designs – one for a dance
outfit, the other for a post
office manager – from a
competition organized to
promote the Men's Dress
Reform Party in London
in 1937.

evaporation of perspiration. He also believed
that wearing wool next to the skin encouraged
the body to 'self-clean' as dead skin scales were
sloughed off. Dr Jaeger's views, though not
scientifically accurate, were nevertheless taken
very seriously: among the numerous customers
at the Jaeger shop in Regent Street, London –
which is still doing fine business today although
it no longer sells 'hygienic dress' – were
progressive intellectuals including George
Bernard Shaw. Adherents to hygienic dress
continued to wear their natural undyed wool
suits right through the twentieth century.
Although Dr Jaeger's knickerbocker suits failed

to oust trousers as the preferred pants for the
man about town, in the countryside and, in
particular, on the golf course, they reigned
supreme. 'Natural' woollen clothing and
'healthy' outdoor country life continue to be
associated to this day.

For many others, reform in dress was
inextricably linked with contemporary politics.
Although widespread mass production meant
that being fashionable was no longer exclusive to
the wealthy, with other sections of society
expressing their social mobility through the
acquisition of fashionable clothes, differences in
class position could still be determined by the

Kier Hardie rejected the morning suit and top hat and entered the House of Commons in 1892 wearing a plain black 'working suit' that was to be the Labour Party uniform throughout the twentieth century.

quality of fabric and the cut and the finish of the clothing that was worn.

Rejecting morning suits, frock coats and evening dress as 'upper-class uniform', the Socialist man adopted the plain black working suit with a double-breasted, tail-less jacket that had been worn by the British Labour Party's first parliamentary MP, Kier Hardie, in 1892. In working suit and a tweed cap Hardie entered a House of Commons populated by men in frock coats and silk top hats. While the press made a fuss and Hardie received gifts of cloaks and toppers, he refused to wear them and the black suit became the Labour Party's uniform, worn by members of parliament and their supporters right through the twentieth century.

Aspiring to more radical change were European avant-garde artists including the Italian Futurists and the Russian Constructivists. In May 1914 the Italian painter Giacomo Balla signed the first manifesto of Futurist Men's Fashions, which declared war on the established

norms of stylishness. Elegance and fashion were, according to Futurists, henceforward to be considered obsolete concepts. In a restatement of the Hygienic Dress ideas, Futurist clothing was to be healthy clothing. According to their manifesto, clothing was to be cut in such a way in order to allow the body to 'breathe'. Consequently, war was declared by the Futurists on heavy fabrics, starched collars, useless decorative details (such as extra buttons on the cuffs) and any garment that impeded body movement. Furthermore, the 'boring niceness', or what the Futurists called the 'neutrality', of contemporary, conformist and class-ridden dress was attacked in the 'Anti-Neutral Clothes' manifesto of September 1914. Instead of the muted colours of mainstream men's clothing, the Futurists advocated clothing that was colourful and asymmetrical. Jackets would have one rounded tail and one square one; the fronts of jackets would no longer have a straight line of buttons: instead jackets would fasten on one side or even up the back. Shoes were to be 'Dynamic' – each a different colour and shape to 'deliver merry kicks to all neutralists', as the manifesto declared. The Futurist painter Gino Severini had often worn one red and one green shoe since 1911. Furthermore instead of the usual neutralist practice of investing in a suit to 'last a lifetime' the Futurists declared that clothing should be short-lived: a concept more usually associated with women's fashions but one that would increasingly affect menswear as well.

The Italian Futurists continued their attacks on conventional dress throughout the 1920s and 1930s issuing a stream of manifestos including ones on hats and metallic ties. Meanwhile, in Paris, the details of the garments worn by the 'dress reformers' who belonged to the circle surrounding the avant-garde artists Robert Delaunay and his wife Sonia Terk were allegedly cabled back to Milan and the Italian Futurists by Severini, their 'artist in residence' in Paris. Described as 'Simultaneist' rather than Futurist, Delaunay was reported to have worn a red cloak with a blue collar, green jacket, a red tie and black and yellow shoes all at the same time. On the whole, however, such attacks on conservative dress remained class-ridden since Futurist and Simultaneist dress was, by and large, confined to educated, middle-class young men.

One garment, however, stands out at this time as a potential outfit that could be worn by everyone: young or old, rich or poor, even male or female. In addition to designing completely new garments such as the *toraco* (a sleeveless shirt) and the *radielfo* (a helmet fitted with radio receivers in the hinged ear flaps) in post-First World War Italy, Ernesto Thayaht designed the *tuta*, an all-in-one, button-through, belted jump-suit. The *tuta* was similar to the clothing experiments that were being conducted in the Soviet Union by the Constructivists, in particular by Alexander Rodchenko, who believed that clothing for the new Soviet man

While Hardie expressed his solidarity with the working man through his clothes, others, like the Dada artist Marcel Duchamp, preferred to express avant-garde artistic ideas or their individuality.

should be comfortable and practical. But Rodchenko believed that every function, or type of work, had its own 'uniform', and therefore each garment or uniform would vary depending on the type of work that was undertaken. Even in the classless Soviet Union, 'difference' between types or classes of workers would continue to be marked by clothing.

While menswear in the twentieth century has been marked by the widespread adoption of clothing originally designed as workwear, these garments – for example, denim jeans, checked 'Lumberjack' shirts and Dr Martin's boots and shoes – have generally passed from one role to the other via an intermediate stage as leisurewear. Thayaht's *tuta* is all the more remarkable in that, as well as being the first all-purpose garment – perhaps the first 'universal' garment – it was the first deliberate attempt to transform workwear directly into everyday wear without such an intermediate stage.

# The Jazz Age

Edward, Prince of Wales was the heir to King George V of England's throne. Like his grandfather Bertie at the turn of the century, Edward was to be a significant figure in the development of men's fashions. Edward was born in 1894 and in May 1936, on the death of his father, became Edward VIII. One of his first acts as king was to abolish the black frock coat at court functions. Edward's fashion decrees at court were short-lived: by December 1936 he put an end to the controversy surrounding his intention to marry Wallis Simpson (an American divorcee and a commoner) by abdicating the throne. The ex-king and his wife assumed the titles of the Duke and Duchess of Windsor and in 1960 the Duke would publish *A Family Album*, an account of his and previous British monarchs' roles in creating new fashions.

In 1920 the Prince of Wales was 26 years old: old enough for his fashion initiatives to be seen as informed yet young enough for him to be regarded by the post-war generation as a rebel against the formality in dress epitomized by his father. The Prince became a leading example of the motto of the new generation: Dress Soft. The majority of his clothes emphasized comfort and freedom of movement: sweaters, soft collars and wide trousers with large pockets – the Prince no doubt remembered the dress restrictions of his years at naval academies where trouser pockets were banned.

The shirt collar was to be the subject of one of the most fiercely-debated issues in men's clothing in the 1920s. Was it supposed to be soft and attached permanently to the shirt or stiff and detachable? Supporters of the stiff collar saw it as the last bastion against the slovenly, casual manner of dress, believed to be the 'American' style of dress, that they felt was undermining the ideals of British male elegance. At a time when the American economy was booming and America's impact on European culture was growing, it is not surprising that many felt under threat. The soft collar won the day and became part of everyday wear. In summer it was even worn without a tie, unbuttoned and draped wide across the jacket lapels in what was known as a Byron collar. At night, where wing collars remained chic with tails, an attached, semi-stiff, turned-down collar found an ally in the dinner jacket or tuxedo.

Above: The overall silhouette of this group of men's clothes is very similar: the working men being addressed by the Prince of Wales have no doubt put on their 'Sunday best'. Only the flat cap of the man standing third from the right betrays his social status.

Left: Even with what appears at first glance to be two almost identically dressed men – on the left, Prime Minister Lloyd George, on the right, the Prince of Wales – distinctions are visible in the details. Note the Prince's more modern soft, turned-down 'American' collar, informally knotted tie and the cut and fit of his suit.

Iin this photograph taken in 1915, Edward Wyndham Tennant wears a double-breasted suit and a striped shirt which has a separate low double collar, made in a fabric matching the shirt.

LE JAZZOFLUTE
ROBE DU SOIR, DE BEER

Nº 2 de la Gazette du Bon Ton.

Année 1922. — Planche 15

The Jazz Age, synonymous with the 'anything goes' Roaring Twenties, still required the correct, formal dress in polite society.

## Baggy Trousers

1925 saw the arrival of Oxford Bags, broad, pleated trousers which were worn by undergraduates at the English university. These soon replaced the slim trousers worn by most young men and the fashion for looser-fitting trousers would last until the advent of denim jeans 30 years later.

Oxford Bags were not a new invention: for some time they had been worn by athletes as an alternative to golf trousers which had been banned in the classroom. The 28" wide bottoms of the Oxfords allowed the trousers to be pulled over the top of their illegal knickers. The original functional size of the hems soon became overlooked as Oxford Bags grew in size, sometimes up to 10" in diameter! Trend-setting Ivy League students brought the fashion home after their stays in Oxford and ordered more pairs from their tailors.

The dominance of loose trousers as city wear was, in fact, partly due to the rise in popularity of sport, in particular, golf. The fashionable golf trousers of the inter-war period were 'plus-fours', a version of the knickerbockers but with a fuller

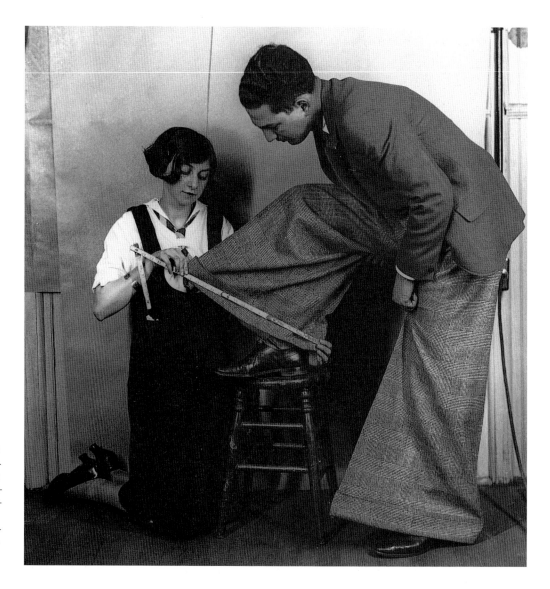

1925 marks the year that Oxford bags were born, replacing the slim trousers worn by most young men. For the next 30 years, loose-fitting trousers would remain the fashionable fit. The comfortable functional aspect of the original 28-inch hems could be lost in grossly oversized versions as much as 40 inches in diameter.

cut that allowed the fabric to fall 4" below the knees, thus giving them their name. Their success led the way for widely-worn suits that were 'sporty' though no longer worn exclusively for sport but also for strolls in the park on Sundays, for travelling and even by the young in town. Once again it was the Prince of Wales who helped popularize plus-fours. A great golfer, the Prince also liked roomy jackets: it was said that the shoulders of his jackets were cut half an inch wider than really necessary. This was no doubt necessary since the Prince is also credited with

wearing pullovers under his loud checked tweeds as sportswear.

The Prince was an ambassador for British fashion and fabrics, particularly in America during his trips in 1924 and 1927 where the American press reported on his dress from top to bottom every day. His penchant for easy-going clothes struck a chord with youthful Americans and, in exchange, he adopted the American fashion of wearing belts rather than braces with his trousers. By the outbreak of the Second World War, while the Prince continued to have

Walter Hagen at the U.S. Open Golf Championships in 1928 at the Winged Foot Golf Club, Mamaroneck, N.Y. sporting the latest in plus fours. A fuller version of the knickerbockers, plus fours derived their name from the fact that the fabric fell four inches below the knee.

The Ambassador for British fashion and fabrics abroad, the Prince of Wales relaxes during a tour of South Africa in 1925.

his jackets tailored in London, it was New York that supplied his trousers. The Dutch firm of Frederick Scholte of No.3 Cork Street in London was the Prince's tailor for 40 years. Scholte was extremely fussy, especially about his clientele: film stars, theatrical performers and 'arrivistes' were banned from entry. Scholte shared many attitudes to men's dress with the Prince's father, George V: neither approved of soft dressing and Scholte was ferocious in his contempt for Oxford Bags and loosely-fitting trousers.

## Bright Days, Bright Knits

The 1920s saw the beginning of an infatuation with the pullover, though initially most department stores still confined knitwear to the sports departments. The French defined three types of knitwear. First was *'le sweater'*, made of fine wool, lightweight and the coolest type of knitwear. Next came *'le pullover'*, the name referring to the way in which it was put on over

Artist Duncan Grant in the gardens at Charleston in 1930. Note the loosely fitting trousers and knitted 'pullover'. Originally confined to the sportsfield, knitted jumpers became popular in the 1920s as casual wear for men.

the head, which was slightly heavier and warmer than '*le sweater*'. The thickest, coarsest and heaviest knitted sweater was '*le chandail*' which derived its name from the '*marchands d'ail*' (garlic merchants). This bulky-knit garment was originally worn by vegetable sellers in French markets and was particularly popular with the 'arty' set, Picasso being one of its most famous wearers.

In England the craze for turtleneck and crewneck jerseys was initiated by playwright and actor Noel Coward in his 1924 play, *Vortex*, while Fair Isle knits were made fashionable by the Prince of Wales in 1922 when he wore one on the golf course at St Andrews. The Prince's patronage of the Fair Isle sweater probably helped to save the knitting industry that remains to this day on the small island between the Shetland and Orkney Islands. Fair Isle patterns were believed to have originated from Spanish sailors who were stranded on the island following the defeat of the Spanish Armada in 1588. However, the earliest examples of the rows of geometric and abstract patterns date from the 1870s. Although there were cardigans and crewneck sweaters available, the Prince preferred V-necks and was frequently photographed in his favourite Fair Isle knits.

Two further examples of sports clothing being adopted as everyday wear were the tennis sweater (also known as the cricket sweater) and the tennis shirt. The cream or white cable-knit, V-neck tennis sweater was popularized in the 1920s as pre- and post-match wear by the

American tennis champion Bill Tilden. Around the same time the Prince of Wales could be seen wearing one on informal occasions and his fashion leadership encouraged the sweater's move away from sporting wear. Subsequently, the tennis sweater – basically unchanged since its introduction to the game in the nineteenth century – has remained part of the vocabulary of fashion knitwear.

On the tennis court gentlemen players were at first expected to wear a necktie as well as a long-sleeved, stiff-collar shirt. In 1926, International Champion René Lacoste began wearing a white pique jersey shirt with a small ribbed collar and

short sleeves with ribbed bands that he had designed for his own use. Dubbed 'le Crocodile' by the press in 1923, supposedly after making a bet that involved an alligator-hide suitcase, Lacoste's nickname also illustrated his vigorous and competitive athleticism on the court. Lacoste's friend Robert George drew an alligator that was first embroidered on Lacoste's blazer and, subsequently, in 1926, on the short-sleeved shirt. Following his retirement from the game in 1929 Lacoste decided to market his shirt: it first appeared in France in 1933 and then in America in 1952. Popular not only for tennis because of its functional design – the longer tail at the back

In 1922 the Prince of Wales began a craze for Fair Isle knitted sweaters after he wore one on the golf course. Popularity engendered by Royal patronage probably saved the Scottish islands' industry from extinction and the patterns for posterity.

French tennis champion Rene Lacoste, known as 'le Crocodile' for his vigorous athleticism on the court began marketing his cotton pique tennis shirt with crocodile motif in 1929. Since then it is esti-mated that over 200 million Lacoste shirts have been sold world-wide.

stayed firmly tucked in during even the most energetic games – Lacoste provided a shirt that was comfortable and stylish enough to remain a staple garment in men's (and women's) wardrobes today. Since first being introduced commercially, it is estimated that more than 200 million Lacoste shirts have been sold worldwide, and that number does not include the fakes. It has since become the model for the three-button 'polo' shirt in a rainbow range of cotton pique from designers like Ralph Lauren and the more 'formal' alternative to the T-shirt.

## Easy Tweeds

The 1920s' obsession with 'dressing soft' extended to fabrics. In 1925's *The Great Gatsby*, F. Scott Fitzgerald had Gatsby open his wardrobe from which he: 'took out a pile of shirts and began throwing them, one by one, before us, shirts of sheer linen and thick silks and fine flannel checks which lost their folds as they fell . . . the rich, soft heap mounted higher'.

At the races in 1925: note the short 'bum-freezer' length of the jackets.

Woollen fabrics reigned supreme, particularly in gaudy checks and stripes that bear the names of their places of origin: Cheviot, Shetland, Donegal and Harris. Originally used for country clothes, these woollens became associated with the healthy outdoor lifestyle and the 1920s saw an increase in outdoor activities such as hiking, mountaineering and Youth Hostelling. The fabrics were ideally suited to these activities: the coarse Cheviot tweeds were thornproof while the 'Homespun' wools produced in cottage industries were water-resistant because the wool still had its natural coating of grease.

'Tweed' is a corruption of 'tweel', a word which for centuries referred to the hand-woven woollen cloth produced by Scottish Highlanders and Islanders. Later it became associated with the River Tweed which divides England and Scotland. Eventually 'tweed' became the general term for all homespun wools whether from Scotland, like Harris

Summer sporting wear in England meant white flannel trousers and blazers. Since the English summer is invariably cool and cricket a notoriously slow game, woollen trousers were – and continue to be – an absolute must for players and spectators!

Tweed, or from Ireland, like Donegal Tweed.

So popular was Harris Tweed that by the end of the 1920s the Harris Tweed Association registered its own trademark in an effort to help consumers differentiate between the real and the fake: unlicensed copying was not restricted to the 1980s and 1990s. Every three yards, the Harris Tweed device, a Maltese Cross topped by a globe, was, and continues to be, stamped on the back of the cloth. This mark guarantees that this true Harris Tweed has been made of pure virgin wool from Scotland that has been spun, dyed in mixtures of heather, seaweeds and lichens scraped from rocks and finished in the Outer Hebridean Islands of Lewis-Harris, Uist and Barra before being woven in strands two by two to produce a uniquely dense yet supple fabric.

The quality of the colour and the cloth means that Harris Tweed was, and is, by no means an inexpensive fabric. It remains popular today for new garments and in bespoke tailoring, but 'vintage' tweeds are also sought out as the all-purpose, all-weather jacket becomes softer and increasingly beautiful the more it is worn.

The other leading fabric of the 1920s was flannel. From the Welsh word 'gwlanen' meaning simply 'woollen cloth', flannel was first used in the nineteenth century for underwear – short and long johns, vests and night-shirts – but by the end of the century was popular for sporting clothes, in particular cricket and tennis trousers. By the early years of the twentieth century, flannel trousers, particularly in white or cream, had been adopted as summer leisurewear, and by the 1920s white flannels worn with plain navy blazer jackets were to be seen at all the seaside resorts and in the movie magazines showing the stars 'at home'. Despite the fragile nature of the cloth – flannel often went baggy, shiny and discoloured when worn for long periods – demand meant it was available in a range of

colours. One of the overriding images of menswear in the 1920s is of the young man casually and softly dressed in white flannel trousers, a white open-neck shirt, a brightly striped flannel blazer and a straw boater.

## Bright Young Things

In addition to the softening of menswear were numerous attempts to increase the amounts of colour worn by men: loud colours combined in different patterns of checks and stripes, brightly striped blazers, gaudy diamond-patterned sweaters and even ties of regiments to which the wearers may never have belonged. The Guards' tie was immensely popular in America: Ernest Hemingway noted that F. Scott Fitzgerald, the author of *The Great Gatsby*, was wearing one with a button-down collar when the pair met in Paris in 1925. English actor Jack Buchanan set the rage for midnight blue evening jackets in the revue *A to Z* in 1927 while novelist Arnold Bennett was an even keener advocate of colour in menswear: although he stuck to black and white for evening dress, Bennett was often seen in London wearing a mauve suit. More extreme was the painter Walter Sickert, who favoured exceptionally loud often unmatching checked suits and large white bowler hats. There were some things, however, that not even the Prince of Wales could get away with: arriving in France at the end of the decade, the Prince stepped from his plane in a pink shirt, regimental striped tie, checked suit, red-and-white checked socks and black-and-tan shoes! The next day the pink shirt and the checked socks were gone.

Outerwear was not the only area to benefit from the new attitudes to fabrics and colour: night attire and underwear were also to undergo transformation. Silk and cotton boxer shorts began to replace woollen 'combinations' or long johns while pyjamas in percale, crepe or silk

POUR VOYAGER

The 1920s passion for dressing soft extended to fabrics and to patterns and colours: tweed reigned supreme. Often in gaudy checks and bright stripes when new, the colours soften and fade to the subtle tones of the countryside.

signalled the end of the flannel night-shirt. One garment usually associated with night attire – the dressing gown – was in the 1920s often a luxurious full-length silk, velvet or brocade affair that was worn to relax in at home in the evenings after men had removed their jackets.

## The Bubble Bursts

The 1920s was marked by an economic prosperity where production and consumer spending were at an all-time high. Unfortunately, this sense of economic security was to be short-lived. As instalment buying became popular, so much credit was extended that there were no longer sufficient funds to back it up. In the stockmarket a buyer needed only to raise 10 per cent of the share price in order to purchase stock.

When the price of stocks rose, the shares in it could be sold at a profit. This went on until 3 September 1929 when the stockmarkets hit an unbelievable high. Then came the fast decline: in less than one month the market value of shares on Wall Street dropped by $30 billion and American unemployment rose from 1.5 million to nearly 13 million as business profits plunged from $10 billion to $2 billion. With nearly half of the nation's banks forced into closure, the Wall Street Crash set off a chain reaction that put the whole world into a severe economic depression.

The garment industry and the fashion trade struggled in the face of a shrinking number of clients each with a newly tightened budget. The 'Bright Young Things' of the 1920s were to grow up in the 1930s and enter an age dominated by social, economic and political turmoils – turmoils that would be reflected in their clothing.

# Heroes, Hunks and Hoodlums

The economic restrictions faced by both consumers and producers of menswear during the Depression set off a trend for simple and sensible dressing. At its extreme, this meant the 'poor look' was in vogue amongst the avant-garde set who even threw 'poverty parties' where guests were invited to dress 'down at heel'. Outside this rarefied atmosphere, however, it was apparent that the social rituals of dress – in particular the habit of changing clothes at different times of the day – were on the way out. Even the most stylish of men might now expected to go out to work and earn a living.

The serious business of work in the 1930s was matched by the sobriety of the business suit, a development of the lounge suit. Whether single or double-breasted, the business suit was dark and even the names of the colours in which it was available matched the essential, even elemental, nature of work: steel grey, charcoal grey, slate blue. Enlivening the potential drabness and plainness, however, were herringbone weaves, checks and vertical stripes. The latter could be single, double or even triple stripes, pin stripes or chalk stripes and were seen to lengthen and enhance the male silhouette. The most stylish of the checks or plaid weaves was Glen Plaid (or Glen Urquart, because of its Scottish origins). Also known as Prince of Wales Check, this pattern owed its popularity to the future King Edward VIII. Originally woven in saxony wool, its intersecting vertical and horizontal lines over a hound's-tooth weave soon appeared in a wide range of materials including tweeds and worsteds like serge and gabardine, hard-wearing woollen fabrics made from smooth yarns. For tailors, Prince of Wales Check was difficult to work with: in order to allow for any imperfections in the weave and because the checks had to be matched up at the seams, shoulders, sleeves and across the legs, three-and-a-half metres of fabric were required instead of the three metres used to make up a plain suit. The slightest cutting or fitting error would be glaringly obvious and consequently more time was needed to perfect the suit. This additional fabric and time involved naturally made Prince of Wales Check suits particularly

The well-dressed man was required to wear appropriate clothes for the time of day (morning suits, evening dress) as well as for particular activities like motoring or relaxing at home. Here mannequins display men's fashions for 1929 at the Great Nottingham Co-operative Society Showroom.

# Three Guardsmen . . . . . a handsome, sturdy herringbone, 1932 (and '33) quality . . . at a 1916 price

WITH our left hand we jammed the lever marked "price" back to the low of sixteen years ago; with our right, we yanked the lever marked "quality" forward hard—farther than it has been in twenty years! Three Guardsmen is the first result: a handsome, firm herringbone worsted weave—tested *seven* ways—at a new low price—the same type of fabric that is most worn by men who needn't care how much they pay. You can have any two of Three Guardsmen for what *one* equally-good-looking suit cost a year or so ago; and all Three Guardsmen for less than the price you used to pay for two such! The three styles shown here are by no means all. You'll admire their tailoring . . . the linings . . . the smooth modeling as the pure worsted yarns are "worked" to drape easily on you. And you'll yelp with relief at the way Guardsmen cut your pressing bills—they *hold* their shape!

© 1932, H. S. & M.

# HART SCHAFFNER & MARX CLOTHES

expensive – and no doubt more desirable. The pattern is notoriously difficult to wear – it makes short men appear even shorter – but flatters the tall, lean and athletic body.

Thanks to the business suit, men's urban dress became more simple and was no longer informed by nineteenth-century etiquette. The pleasure-seeking 'dandies' were now completely vanquished; in their place was the new, 'tough' modern man.

Far left: The serious business of work in the 1930s was matched by the sobriety of the 'business suit'. By the depression years of the 1930s, the ritual of changing one's clothes through the day was largely passing.

Centre: The Prince of Wales in a Glen Urquart check which became popularly known as 'Prince of Wales Check'.

Cabinet Minister Samuel Hoare in 1938, in a lounge suit (with no turn-ups) and bowler hat, carrying a rolled umbrella and gloves.

## A Cut Above the Rest

The acknowledged master of men's tailoring in the 1930s was Frederick Scholte, tailor to the Prince of Wales, who popularized a cutting technique known as the 'Drape cut' or the 'London cut'. Scholte was the first London tailor to apply the principles used in the tailoring of military uniforms for the officers of the Royal Household Guards to civilian dress. Scholte

Savile Row, London remains the home of bespoke tailoring. Here tailor Lionel Birch fits trousers for his client who prefers the English style of braces (suspenders) over the American fashion for belted waists.

admired the broad-shouldered athletic image projected by the guards – particularly when they wore their greatcoats – and it was this cut and drape that he adapted for his clients. Officers' greatcoats were wide-shouldered and high-belted while fine horizontal drapes narrowed as they fell from the arms to the waist. Combined, these elements gave an inverted triangle silhouette: broad at the top and narrowing towards the bottom. While many of these details had already been incorporated into the masculine profile, Scholte's Savile Row pedigree and the royal patronage of his 'London cut' gave the silhouette authority both in Europe and, in particular, in America where the Prince of Wales was an acknowledged leader in men's fashion.

## Chests Out, Shoulders Back!

The look of the 'Bright Young Things' was too soft – effeminate even – for the climate of the 1930s and consequently a harder and squarer silhouette became considered the epitome of masculinity. Interest in sport in the late 1920s had already contributed to changing the physical build of men and by the 1930s the 'ideal' male body entailed wide shoulders, straight backs, narrow hips and flat stomachs.

For some the idea of the physically perfect male body was linked with the political ideologies of Nazi Germany and Fascist Italy. The Berlin Olympics of 1936 was to be notable for Hitler's attempt to turn the event into a display of Aryan superiority. When Jesse Owens broke two world records and carried away four gold medals it made a mockery of the Reich's racial ideologies and Hitler refused to present champion Owens with his medals.

Most men, however, simply saw the effect that the rippling torso of former Olympic

swimming champion turned Hollywood actor, Johnny Weissmuller (who played the eponymous hero in the Tarzan movies from 1932) had on his female fans. Weissmuller was not the only idol to bare his chest: in 1934 Clark Gable changed the face of men's underwear when he took off his shirt in *It Happened One Night* to reveal a vestless chest. American sales reputedly dropped by 30 per cent. On the tennis court, American champion Bunny Austin, after a two-year battle with his

Tennis champion Bunny Austin first stepped on to the court in shorts in 1932. At the time such attire for professional players was unheard of but by the end of the decade most players had adopted the 'ventilated pants', as the press dubbed them.

By 1930, the double-breasted jacket was the height of male elegance. The most popular versions had large broad lapels which accentuated the square cut of the shoulders.

self-consciousness, stepped on to the court at the 1932 US Men's Championships at Forest Hills, New York in shorts. Such attire was unheard of and even the porter at Austin's hotel before the match whispered in his ear: 'Excuse me Mr Austin, but I think you've forgotten your trousers!'

For those men who did not and could never have the body of a Gable or a Weissmuller, shoulder pads, raised arm holes and sleeves which narrowed at the wrists to give the illusion of broad shoulders aided the creation of the square and wide-shouldered look. The most useful devices for broadening

Major Casey in a double-breasted suit. The DB jacket was slightly longer than its 'sportier' cousin, the single-breasted jacket and placed less emphasis on the waist, thus creating a squarer, broader shouldered look.

the chest were peaked or pointed lapels and the wearing of double-breasted jackets.

Related to the nautical pea-jacket or reefer jacket, double-breasted jackets played only a limited role in men's wardrobes before the First World War. Subsequently, the double-breasted jacket began to do battle with its single-breasted 'sportier' cousin as the appropriate style for city clothes and by 1930, the DB (double-breasted) jacket was the height of male elegance. The most popular version had large, broad lapels which accentuated the square-cut shoulders, six buttons (in two rows of three) and fell to straight, ventless tails which hugged the hips. Following the popularity of the Scholte 'London cut', four-buttoned DB suits with lapels that sloped down towards the bottom buttons and a slightly lengthened jacket that placed less emphasis on the waist were widespread. This version, associated with the Prince of Wales and his younger brother, the Duke of Kent, was first known as a 'Kent DB' and later as a 'Windsor DB' after the Prince's abdication of the throne and his assumption of the title of the Duke of Windsor. The DB suit was finished off with long, wide trousers which aimed to give the wearer a tall, 'column'-like appearance.

The ultimate in modern trousers were those that had zips. Whitcomb Judson, a Chicago inventor, had first introduced a metal 'slide' fastener in 1891 but it took some fine tuning before a practical fastener could be made on the now familiar tape fabric backing. In 1923 the B.F. Goodrich Company first used the term 'zipper' to describe the fastener but for the most part its use was confined to luggage until around 1934 when the Prince of Wales, George, Duke of York and Lord Louis Mountbatten gave it royal approval by appearing in public in trousers with zip flies. Many men were suspicious of the zip's ability

to defy gravity, and button flies survived through the Second World War. Nevertheless, the zip did spread to other garments like sweaters and jackets, where they were often used decoratively. On trousers, however, until some of the wilder fashions of the 1960s and 1970s, zips on trousers continued to be concealed by the fly front.

## Hooray for Hollywood!

Promising 'two chickens in every pot and two cars in every garage', on 4 March 1933 Franklin Delano Roosevelt became the 32nd President of the United States and launched the New Deal, a programme of political and economic initiatives designed to lift the country out of the Depression. By 1935 there were signs of recovery and FDR's campaign song 'Happy Days Are Here Again' seemed to be being fulfilled.

In menswear American stylishness was to reign supreme: so much so that by the end of the decade the 'London cut' would be renamed the 'American cut' without any recriminations from the tailors of Savile Row. The widespread acceptance of the American way of dressing was greatly assisted by the images projected by the Hollywood film industry in the 1930s and 1940s.

Unlike the female stars, whose wardrobes were designed for them, and with the exception of historical costumes, male actors were expected to provide their own wardrobes. In some instances contracts stipulated that the studios' own tailors were to be used while the leading male stars were allowed to commission their own tailors and offset the costs against the studios' expenses. The result was that the clothes worn on-screen by male film stars had an 'immediacy' in terms of fashion that could be admired and emulated by their fans.

Hollywood's British-born actors – Ronald Colman, Leslie Howard, Herbert Marshall, Noel

This advert for Jaeger Coats (1935) shows the ideal male body style of the period: tall, square-shouldered and tapering to the ankles like an inverted triangle.

Top: Hollywood star and one of the world's best dressed men, Cary Grant was a customer at Savile Row tailors Kilgour, French and Stanbury. Always conscious of his appearance, Grant had his jackets padded at the shoulders.

Below: Fred Astaire relaxing at his Hollywood home. Astaire 'tested' his Savile Row suits by walking up and down Bond Street in them. To achieve his signature look of casual elegance, Astaire is reputed to have thrown his clothes at walls to knock out their newness.

A young Gary Cooper shapes up
for future Hollywood stardom. In
the 1930s the ideal male body was
tall, lean and athletic.

In Howard Hawks' film *Scarface* (1931) Paul Muni (standing, wearing light hat and light tie) portrayed a bootlegging gangster based on the figure of Al Capone. Muni's costume of DB suit with exaggerated lapels spawned a fashion for gangster-style clothes, particularly among young working class 'toughs'.

Coward and Jack Buchanan – crossed and re-crossed the Atlantic on the 'last word in luxury' ocean liners with at least 20 pieces of matching luggage containing sufficient clothes for the 8 or 9-day crossing. The reason for their London visits: Savile Row. Jack Buchanan had been one of the few celebrity clients at Scholte's since the 1920s, while one Archibald Leach – better known as Cary Grant – had his suits made at Kilgour, French and Stanbury. An impeccable dresser both on and off screen, Grant is reputed to have quipped about his film roles: 'I play only myself, but I play it to perfection.' Not surprisingly Grant's suits were heavily padded at the shoulders to make his head appear smaller! Fred Astaire had shopped on Savile Row sine the 1920s, though

not always with success. Astaire's first London performance was in the 1923 revue *Stop Flirting*. It was a huge success; even the Prince of Wales went backstage to congratulate the cast. Astaire was so impressed by the Prince's clothes that, learning that the Prince had his dress shirts and vests made by Hawes and Curtis, he raced over to order exactly the same the next day only to be told that this was not possible. Astaire had run into the superior attitude of the royal outfitters who flatly refused to dress anyone from show business. He had better luck at the firm of Anderson and Sheppherd, who although not 'By Royal Appointment', were, at least, in Savile Row. Astaire, so concerned with his appearance that he allegedly 'tested' his suits before he bought them by going for a walk down Bond Street, was reputed to throw new clothes at the wall several times to 'knock out' the newness to achieve his signature style of 'casual elegance'.

Representative of the other end of the spectrum of Hollywood men's fashions was Spencer Tracy, whose movie roles as a 'man of the people' fostered a style of mis-matched tweeds and checked patterns while James Stewart's informal look of V-neck sweater and cuffed pants was to become standard dress for many Joe Colleges on American campuses in the 1930s.

One style of dress from Hollywood that did not find favour with high society but which, nevertheless, was adopted by many young men was the slouched manner of the gangsters: both the real-life hoods and their movie representations. Paul Muni portrayed a bootlegging gangster based on Al Capone in Howard Hawks' *Scarface* (1931). Muni's costume of double-breasted suit with exaggerated lapels and hat pulled down over one eye set the trend for numerous copies which were popular particularly with young, working-class men. For the first time the 'lower classes' were not following the dress patterns set by 'upper-class' role models. This revolt against accepted good taste and stylishness was to be halted by the outbreak of the Second World War, and fashion would have to wait until the advent of the teenager in the 1950s to pick up the threads of this first 'revolt into style'.

## Fun in the Sun

American fashion was to impact in another area of menswear: summerwear. The popular resorts of Newport, Palm Springs, Palm Beach and Nassau in the Bahamas were where the rich and fashionable could be seen soaking up the sun during the inter-war period. Thanks to

the movies and movie magazines which featured the stars relaxing in summer resort wear and the arrival of wealthy Americans 'doing Europe', summer fashions spread from the New World to the old. The vogue for fitness, outdoor sports and leisure activities and, above all, a sun-tanned body, transformed the former winter season resorts of the French Riviera – Cannes, Nice and Monte Carlo – into summertime hot-spot destinations.

One of the most popular outfits for summerwear was the 'Palm Beach suit' named after the famous Florida resort. The Palm Beach suit could be either a 'Kent DB' or single-breasted, but rather than having the peaked lapels of the business suit, the Palm Beach had open-notched lapels (or, as they were known in Europe, 'American lapels'). Its success was not so much to do with the cut but the materials out of which Palm Beach suits were made: lightweight, tropical fabrics like seersucker, shantung and linen.

Seersucker, the name derived from the Persian '*shiroshakkar*', meaning 'milk and honey', is a puckered cotton fabric that was imported from India. Two layers of yarn – one taut, the other loose – are woven in vertical alternations to give seersucker its characteristic stripe and naturally 'crinkled' appearance. Initially seersucker had been used in the southern states of America as a fabric for workwear, but it was much appreciated for its coolness and lightness.

Shantung is a more expensive fabric made from Chinese wild silk. It creases easily, particularly in hot, humid climates. Nevertheless, ecru or natural-coloured shantung and linen jackets were very desirable despite the availability of new lightweight synthetic fabrics. These jackets were worn with wide beach slacks or Bermuda shorts, and when sports shoes like canvas deck or boating shoes weren't worn, then 'Norwegian slippers' were popular. These soft shoes, better known

Here are a few of the many holiday necessities and luxuries to be seen at Austin Reed's of Regent Street. With the sixth floor as headquarters, we have a quite dazzling array of sports kit of every kind and colour.

**AUSTIN REED LIMITED 103-113 REGENT STREET LONDON WI**

Far left: American fashions impacted on many areas of European menswear, including summer clothes. Fan magazines showing the movie stars relaxing at home or in the sunshine resorts of Palm Springs or the Bahamas spread styles from the New World to the Old and were soon reinforced by new menswear magazines like *Apparel Arts* and *Esquire*.

Left: The vogue for fitness and outdoor sports and leisure activities encouraged many men to extend their wardrobe beyond their business suit, shirt and tie into a whole new range of sports and leisure outfits.

to us today as loafers, began their life as Indian moccasins and somehow crossed the Atlantic and North Sea to Norway where young American tourists 'rediscovered' them in the 1930s. Manufactured in America by G.H. Bass and Co. in 1936, the 'Bass Weejun' (i.e. Norwegian) penny loafer – which got its name from the habit of placing a penny in the 'slot' of the vamp – were to become standard footwear for generations of college kids. Today the Bass Weejun loafer ranks as one of the Great American Classics of fashion.

The fun in the sun mentality encouraged the heightened sense of body consciousness and, consequently, designers began to cut away at swimwear. During the 1920s men had worn one-piece swimsuits which covered their chests: those who uncovered their chests on public beaches risked arrest by the police for indecency. By 1932, however, the European craze at private beaches for swimming without shirts gained momentum and men began to cast off their shirts. A variety of swimsuit styles in the 1930s offered male swimmers solutions to the problems posed by the laws regarding decent dress on public beaches: the Jantzen 'Topper' model of 1934 incorporated the new fastening device – a zipper at the waist – that allowed for the attachment of the swim shirt when decorum ruled. Soon, however, swim shirts for men would disappear and designers began to alter the shape of the remaining trunks by cutting the legs higher. New elastic fabrics like Lastex promised a better figure-hugging fit, and one which stayed even after the fabric was wet.

## Read All About It!

The mass media in the 1930s undoubtedly played an important role in the dissemination of men's fashion and the decade saw the launch of *Apparel Arts* and *Esquire*.

In an effort to promote fashion consciousness in both the industry and the public, in 1931 Abby Gingrich launched *Apparel Arts*, the first male fashion magazine to be aimed at the 'trade': the manufacturers, wholesalers and retailers of men's fashions. Two years later Gingrich launched *Esquire*, this time a menswear magazine aimed at the general public which, by 1937, had more than 700,000 subscribers. Taking his cue from President Roosevelt, Gingrich believed that men's fashion should be 'democratized' and made available to the huge market of middle-class and working class consumers. Unlike some of his European counterparts who featured exclusive custom made clothes in their publications, Gingrich was pioneer of high-quality ready-to-wear clothes – a stand that gave a major boost to the American garment industry that, like Hollywood, was entering a golden age that would last until the 1960s.

A page from menswear magazine *Esquire* which was launched in 1932 by Abby Gingrich. Aimed not at the trade but at the general male public, by 1937 the magazine had over half a million subscribers.

*162*

**ESQUIRE**

*Fashion leaders on the Riviera favor silk net shirts in the new Algerian brown, with half sleeves and open front, worn with light grey shorts and brown and white Norwegian slippers. This outfit is ideal for deck games, luncheon, cocktails, and for wear to and from the cabaña or beach club.*

*The Mexican poncho, made in lightweight terry cloth and other toweling fabrics in the new reed color, supplants the beach robe. It is ideal for lounging on the beach or for use aboard ship as a robe to be worn on deck. Originally worn at St. Tropez, French Riviera.*

*At ports of call in the tropics, lightweight suits of silk, linen, Palm Beach cloth and synthetic fabrics are all-important in the new hemp color. This single breasted model is worn with a tan Madras shirt with lounge collar attached, plain color Shantung silk tie, lightweight hose, reverse calf shoes, and Bombay bowler or pith helmet.*

*A popular outfit at Eden Roc and Cannes last summer was the Algerian brown cabaña coat with carnelian color shorts. Note that the shorts have cuffs like regulation trousers. The sandals are leather blocks in rectangular shape, also making their first appearance on the Riviera.*

*(For answers to all dress queries, send stamped self-addressed envelope to Esquire Fashion Staff, 366 Madison Ave., N.Y.)*

*Robert Goodman*

## SOUTHERN AND CRUISE WEAR

# Fashion at the Front

With the outbreak of the Second World War in 1939 men's fashions were put on hold. In particular, the habit of wearing different clothes at different times of the day could not be sustained. Even in the British armed forces the tradition of full dress, undress and mess uniforms was to come to an end due to the combination of fabric shortages and the increasing numbers of soldiers who required 'kitting out'.

In the first phase of the war, civilians in Britain and France did not face clothing shortages. Ironically it was in Germany where the situation was most acute and the system of rationing and clothing coupons first appeared. In France, clothing coupons were introduced in February 1941 and, following the Fall of France in June that year, the German occupiers issued a decree which regulated the purchase of fabrics and clothes. All French citizens over the age of three years old were allotted with a card worth 100 points. This allowed the purchase of garments according to the official rating of each item.

Although this system was intended to be temporary, it continued until 1944 when a short-sleeved shirt would cost 13 points, a pair of pants, 52 points and a jacket, 67 points. Should you have need of an overcoat, in 1944 it would cost 174 points – nearly two years' worth of clothing allowance. Although the number of points available was increased slightly each year, there were never enough of them to accumulate a wardrobe, the standard of which was set by the German administration at two suits, one knitted vest or pullover, one raincoat or jacket, one pair of winter gloves, one overcoat, three shirts, two undershirts, three pairs of undershorts, two nightshirts, six pairs of socks and six handkerchiefs.

In Britain, clothing rationing was initially considered by the government in June 1940 but was not introduced until June 1941. Initially, the British allowance was 66 coupons per year, but unlike in France, which had an annual increment, by the spring of 1942 the British found their allowances cut to around

48 per year. In 1941; at the start of rationing, a man's overcoat cost 16 coupons, a pair of trousers was 8 coupons and a pair of shoes was 7 coupons. For those who still wished to have their suits made-to-measure, cloth was rationed: one yard of woollen cloth would be 3 coupons. The alternative was the clothing that was not rationed: workmen's boilersuits of the kind worn by Prime Minister Winston Churchill when 'meeting the people' in order to demonstrate his 'common touch', bib and brace overalls and wooden clogs.

In both countries new schemes to manage the shortages were introduced by 1942. In France coats and jackets could no longer have pleated or darted pockets and backs; double-breasted suits were verboten and trousers were limited to a single hip pocket and a maximum ankle width of 10½ inches. Turn-ups or cuffs on trousers – for a long time seen as 'English style' and desirable – were simply banned. In Britain the Utility Scheme was introduced. In order to save labour and to reduce the amount of fabric used, garment styles were simplified,

In June 1941 rationing was introduced in Britain to manage wartime shortages. In 1942, the Utility Scheme was launched. In order to save valuable resources, garment styles were simplified, the number of buttons reduced, the size of pleats and the width of sleeves curtailed and turn-ups on trousers removed.

The War Cabinet. Fourth from the right is Prime Minister Winston Churchill. Front creases in the trousers remain, but turn-ups have been outlawed by the rationing of fabric. All but one of the civilian ministers are wearing single-breasted jackets.

Winston Churchill setting an example by wearing a 'Siren Suit' (overalls).

the Board of Trade forced manufacturers to pay special attention to quality since customers were buying clothes less frequently and so naturally demanded longer-wearing, well-made garments. The Concentration Scheme, also introduced in 1942, allowed only a limited number of approved manufacturers to continue production and barred entry to any newcomers to the clothing industry, a move that no doubt removed many manufacturers at the bottom end of the market.

America was not untouched by the shortages. In 1942 supplies of wool for civilian use were cut by nearly 50 per cent to 136 thousand tons in order to meet the needs of clothing the American army. With wool shortages worldwide, many countries turned to the artificial fibres, viscose and rayon, which were derived from wood pulp. The far-reaching impact of new fibre technology and its effect on fashion would, however, have to wait until peace was won.

Given the climate of rationing and the return of what amounted to sumptuary laws regulating the cut of clothes, one might be forgiven for thinking that new fashion for men would simply die out. In Britain rationing affected everyone: whether you shopped at Savile Row or the local high street, you still had to hand over the same number of coupons. King George VI set the example to 'make do and mend' by continuing to wear his pre-war suits – although for most public ceremonies he wore naval uniform – and when his shirt cuffs and collars became frayed he had them replaced with fabric from his shirt tails. Though not a fashion leader like the Duke of Windsor, the King set an example in a time of acute shortage by applying the strict rationing limits to his own family. Nevertheless, it is fair to say that those men who could afford to have their suits made by

the number of buttons allowed was reduced, the size of pleats and the width of sleeves were curtailed and, once again, turn-ups on trousers were removed. All Utility garments had to be basic and necessary, not fashion 'fads', yet they were in many instances of extremely high quality: all had to pass strict tests for 'value for coupon', shrinkage, colour-fastness and, where appropriate, waterproofness. A testament to the quality of materials and workmanship of these garments is that clothing carrying the Utility label can still be found in second-hand clothing stores. It is most likely that the restrictions introduced by

London's finest gentlemen's outfitters before the war probably found that their clothes did them better service than those who had to rely on cheaper off-the-peg items.

## Zazous and Zoot-suiters

Despite rationing, two groups of men remained defiant when it came to their clothes: the Zoot-suiters in America and the Zazous in France. The word Zoot came from the urban jazz culture of the 1930s but the actual origin of the highly distinctive style adopted by young urban black men on the East Coast and by Mexican immigrants in California is uncertain, although most believe it to have been born around 1935 in Harlem night-clubs such as Sammy's Follies and the Savoy Ballroom. Zoot suits consisted of an over-sized, often double-breasted jacket worn with large padded shoulders and peg-top trousers which narrowed towards the ankle (both of which were extremely draped). Malcolm X was a fifteen-year-old shoeshine boy at the Roseland Ballroom in Boston in 1940 when he bought his first Zoot suit and had his photograph taken to celebrate the event. In his autobiography Malcolm X described his brightly-coloured knob-toed 'kick-up' shoes from Florsheims as the 'ghetto's Cadillac of shoes' and his 'conk' – his hair, straightened at home using dye which often burned the scalp – was bright red. The Zoot-suiter's outfit would be completed by a bright, beautifully hand-painted tie, a coloured pocket handkerchief, a wide-brimmed hat and an extremely long watch chain.

Such suits seemed a deliberate snub to wartime rationing and led to the widespread belief that all Zoot-suiters had links with the criminal underworld and were unpatriotic draft dodgers. In fact many Zoot-suiters were legally

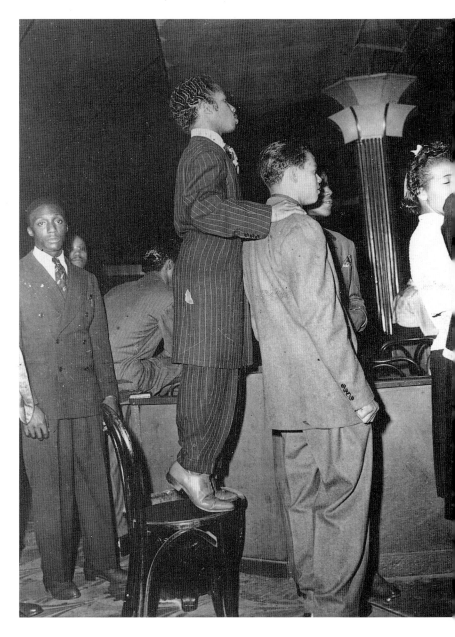

exempt from active duty either on the grounds that they were medically unfit or that they were the sole provider of their family's income. Nevertheless, their highly visible presence was enough to lead to tension, particularly at the naval bases where servicemen were stationed. In what were essentially race riots involving young Blacks, Mexicans and uniformed servicemen, Zoot-suiters saw their clothes as a defiant statement of ethnicity and rebellion from white authority.

Zoot-suiters at the Savoy Ballroom, Harlem. Seemingly in defiance of wartime restrictions, the Zoot-suiter's outfits consisted of oversized, often DB jackets with padded shoulders and draped, peg top trousers. The quantities of fabric needed to construct a zoot suit led to a widespread belief that Zoot-suiters were unpatriotic and had suppliers and contacts in the criminal underworld.

The highly-distinctive style of the zoot-suiter – here, note the long watch chain – found popularity in two groups in America: young urban blacks on the East Coast and, on the West Coast, with young Mexican immigrants. Many zoot-suiters saw their clothes as a defiant statement of ethnicity and rebellion from white culture.

In France the Zazous (the name appears to
have come from the hot-clubs of jazz in Paris
in the late 1930s) were white youths who wore
long jackets with wide, sloping shoulders and
flap pockets which were often made from large
check-patterned fabrics. Their draped trousers,
gathered at the waist, ended in turn-ups or
cuffs a good four inches above the ankle to
display white or brightly-coloured socks and
thick-soled suede shoes. The most elegant
Zazous sported leather open-weave gloves,
wore sunglasses – day and night and at all
times indoors – and carried a Chamberlain
umbrella whether or not it was raining.
Initially the Zazous' style was simply a shift in
fashion but it was during the occupation of
France by the Germans and the ensuing
clothing restrictions that their extravagant use
of fabrics took on the connotations of
rebellion. Because of their very clothing,
Zazous, like the Zoot-suiters, were visible in
their defiance. In 1942, the collaborationist
press condemned the Zazous as lazy and
unpatriotic (i.e. un-German) and the first
'round-ups' and street beatings of Zazous took
place. Gangs of scissor-wielding collaborators
(their ranks no doubt swelled by many
patriotic Frenchmen simply annoyed at the
Zazous' apparent black-market activities)
yelled 'Scalp the Zazous'. This activity did in
fact follow a decree which ordered French
barbers to collect the hair cutting of their
clients which was then mixed with viscose and
made into slippers.

While the styles of both the Zazous and
the Zoot-suiters were to die out as the war
progressed, a refined version of their
silhouette was to become the shape of
menswear in the next decade: wide-shouldered,
long, loose-fitting jackets and high-waisted
tapering pants that were short enough not to
'break' on the shoes.

## I Wore Monty's Duffel

Throughout history, clothing designed
specifically for warfare has, in peacetime, been
adopted by civilians and by the fashion industry.
The cardigan (named after its inventor, the Earl
of Cardigan, who wore the button-through
knitted sweater during the Crimean War) and
the balaclava (named after the Crimean battle)
have found their way into contemporary
wardrobes. Some of today's most popular
garments – T-shirts, trench coats, flying jackets,
bomber jackets, pea-jackets, chino pants and
even Ray Ban's 'Aviator'-style sunglasses – all
have their origins in combatwear.

The modern T-shirt began life as a humble
piece of underwear issued to troops during the
First World War. It was to remain largely unseen
until the 1950s when it was transformed into
outerwear and popularized by Marlon Brandon
and James Dean. The 1960s saw the T-shirt as
unisex wear and a vehicle for political slogans
while in the 1980s it became an advertising
billboard when designers' names were
emblazoned across millions of chests.

The alternative to a wool overcoat, the trench
coat, began life in British-ruled India in the
nineteenth century before it was redesigned for
officers serving in the trenches during the First
World War. After the Armistice in 1918, the
waterproof, woollen-lined trench coat entered
civilian life and was worn by style leaders from
the Prince of Wales to Hollywood stars. Trench
coats appeared to be standard issue for every
movie secret agent, hard-boiled private eye and
journalist in the 1930s and 1940s, with the
ultimate 'hero-in-a-trench coat' being Humphrey
Bogart in *Casablanca* (1942). Today the double-
breasted trench coat with its clear military
origins – epaulets, wrist straps that can be
tightened against the cold and wet and the D-
rings on the belt and yoke that were originally for
carrying grenades – is the signature garment of
companies from Burberry and Aquascutum in

Next page left: The Second World
War inspired military-styled
civilian clothing. Here a 'battle
dress' style jacket is modelled at
the exhibition Modern Men's
Wear at Austin Reed's, the
London outfitters.

Next page right: Rationing continued after hostilities ceased and the
'make do and mend' ethos persist-
ed. Nevertheless, new developments in fibres, fabrics and fashions lifted the spirits. Here an
oiled nylon waterproof suit, which
is small enough to fit into a handy
pouch, is modelled at the Modern
Men's Wear exhibition.

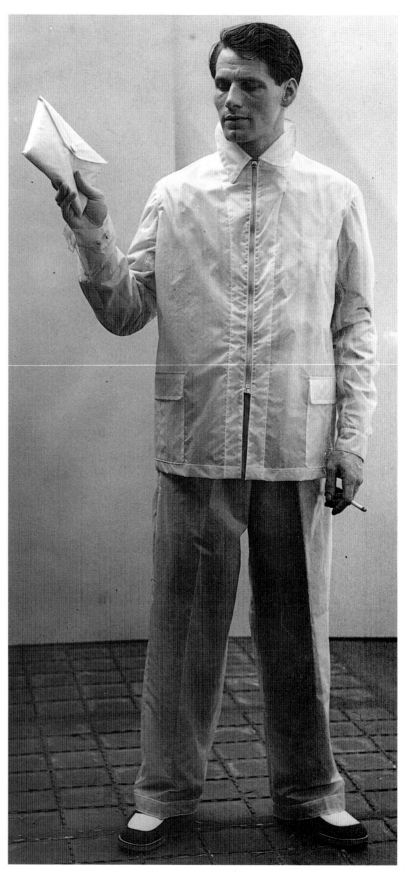

Previous page: Humphrey Bogart in the popular alternative to a woollen overcoat, the trench coat. Standard issue to all Hollywood private eyes, secret agents and journalists, the trench coat is one example of a garment originally designed for military use that has become a fashion item.

Above: Supreme Commander of the Allied Forces, General Dwight D. Eisenhower in the jacket officially designated by the U.S. Army as 'Wool Field Jacket M-1944' but popularly-known as the Eisenhower jacket since it was the one the General preferred to wear when meeting troops in the field.

Right: The flying or bomber jacket made of sheepskin or leather also made the crossover from uniform to fashion after the war.

England to London Fog in America.

Military clothing was highly visible during the war years, not only on soldiers who were home on leave but also in movie images, newsreels and photographs in *Life Magazine* and *Picture Post*. Even after the war reached its end, images of uniform remained steadfast. It was some years before many servicemen returned home and, in Britain, before they were 'de-mobilized' and issued with a 'de-mob' suit – a ready-made suit  issued to all returning servicemen to help them re-start their lives in 'civvy street'. Supreme Commander of the Allied Forces, General Dwight D. Eisenhower returned home in a jacket named after him. The Eisenhower was a fitted waist-length jacket with roomy sleeves and buttoned cuffs that was designed to be carefully poised between 'smart' and 'informal' and was the General's preference when meeting troops in the field. Eisenhower had ordered the design of the 'Wool field jacket M-1944', as it was

Above: Duffel coats on the catwalk. In the hands of contemporary designers, the original coarse wool fisherman's coat, later adopted by the Royal Navy as a deck coat, has been transformed from functional workwear into fashion.

Right: Well into the 1950s men's clothing styles and fabrics continued to be dominated by military influences. Note the selling point: 'Top Quality Army Twill' fabric.

returning home often left their jackets as parting gifts to youths they had befriended, and in August 1945, when America sold off millions of items of army surplus, many young men were able to buy Chinos (so-called because of their point of origin: the fabric was originally woven in Britain, exported to China and then sold to the Americans in the Philippines during the First World War), US Air Force jackets (with high pockets to discourage pilots from putting their hands in them), fatigue jackets and pants. For many young men, these garments were to become their daily clothes.

In the post-war period, military clothing continued to have an impact on menswear both in the wearing of army surplus and in designer versions of military garments. In the 1950s Chinos went to school: worn with loafers, a sweater and a tweed jacket they became the trademark of 'Joe College', a look that would be revived in the 1980s particularly by American designers Calvin Klein and Ralph Lauren. Duffel coats in France after the war became associated with left-wing intellectuals and Existentialism while in Britain they are remembered as school uniform coats until the 1980s when Mulberry, Katharine Hamnett and Hackett raised them to the status of designer 'must-have' that they continue to enjoy today. Meanwhile every young, would-be warrior from 1960s' revolutionaries, through 1970s' Punk to the survivalists, 'Last Action Heroes' and urban street rappers of the last two decades have drafted at least one item of army surplus into their wardrobes.

officially designated by the US Army, as a copy of the jacket worn by British commander, Field Marshall 'Monty' Montgomery and it was issued to American troops in North Africa and Europe in November 1944. It was Monty who also popularized the duffel coat during the Second World War. Named after the Belgian town where the coarse beige wool was woven, the duffel coat was originally fishermen's wear before the British Royal Navy adopted the hooded and large-patch pocket coat with its rope frogging and wooden toggle buttons as an overcoat for sailors on deck watch. Both the Eisenhower and the duffel coat were to become highly prized items of clothing in post-war Europe. Following the Liberation, GIs

# Teens, Teds and Transatlantic Fashions

In the years following the Second World War America was to extend its sartorial suzerainty by virtue of emerging from the conflict as one of the, if not the, most powerful nations on earth. Like her allies, America had sacrificed the lives of many young men but while Europe now spoke of reconstruction and regeneration, rebuilding the fabric of its cities which lay in ruins following bombing raids, America spoke of reconversion, the shifting of its economy from a war to a peacetime footing.

In Britain basic essentials such as bread and fuel were in short supply and rationing of many items was to continue well into the 1950s. Compared with their British cousins, Americans were positively wealthy. By 1947 America was providing around half of the world's total manufacturing output and nearly three quarters of the world's automobiles.

In an effort to redress some of the imbalance between American plenty and European need, US President Harry Truman launched the Marshall Plan. Beginning in 1948, the Plan would spend $17 billion in four years bolstering the economies of all European countries outside the Iron Curtain and Turkey. The Marshall Plan was not simply motivated by good will: without the injection of dollars, potential export markets could face economic collapse. The ensuing chaos in Europe might help to spread a political and economic ideology that was in total opposition to America's own interests: Communism.

In 1951 *Fortune* magazine, in a specialist issue called 'The American Way of Life', declared that American capitalism was 'popular capitalism'. This view was shared by economist J.K. Galbraith, who in his book *America Capitalism* (1952) said simply: 'It works.' The title of Galbraith's subsequent book, *The Affluent Society*, was to become a catch-all phrase to describe the era. In it he wrote that it was indeed production that had done away with the tensions associated with inequality. America would therefore fight the Cold War not only with threats of its nuclear capability but also by exporting its economic, social, political and artistic culture abroad. It would be aided in this effort by the one thing that wasn't in short supply at the end of the war: children.

A 3          A 11          A 10          A 12          A 2          A 8          A 1

Hᴇʀᴇ are illustrations of the full series of our styles in the Stock Block service. Readers will find these stock blocks invaluable for illustrating their local press advertisements, brochures, letterheads, etc. There are at pre-

# STOCK BLOCKS

sent thirteen different styles available which we illustrate individually each week. Blocks

are available 3in. deep by approximately 1in. wide (as illustrated), and priced at 19s. 6d. Readers requiring stock blocks should apply to `` Stock Blocks,'' Tailor and Cutter House, Gerrard Street, London, W.1.

The end of hostilities and the return home of the fighting heroes had, unsurprisingly, led to a huge increase in the birthrate. The result was the advent of a new phenomenon: the teenager, whose impact both in terms of style and as a growing market for fashion would send shock waves around the world.

## The Rise of the Teenager

Although the term 'teener' had existed in the nineteenth century, there had been no real concept of a separate class of youth. Now, in the same breath as the word 'teenager' the phrase 'juvenile delinquent' could often be heard. In May 1956, *The Blackboard Jungle*, with its tale of

Despite the continuation of rationing after the war in Britain, these illustrations of men's styles from *Tailor and Cutter* demonstrate that being well dressed remained a high priority.

Two heroes of popular youth culture Elvis Presley (left) and James Dean (right) helped to establish denim jeans as the uniform of rebellious teenage youth.

teen school rebels, hit London's screens. The soundtrack included Bill Haley and the Comets singing 'Rock Around the Clock' and the young went wild and danced in the aisles. But the impact on dress would not come with the Comets, who on their British tour in 1957 wore rather strange tartan plaid dinner jackets! It was to be *Jailhouse Rock* that determined the course of fashion, and its star, Elvis Presley, was celebrated by millions (and condemned by many for his bad influence on the young). Elvis sparked off the fashion for denim among his fans, leading to a general increased demand for blue jeans.

While denim was not the first workwear fabric to be elevated to fashion, what was new was the huge market for it among the young. Levi Strauss had made jeans for American miners and cowboys since the nineteenth century, and though many cowboys could be seen in westerns at the movies, their jeans were still seen as purely working clothes. In the 1950s, however, following films like *Rebel Without a Cause* (1955), *Giant* (1956) – both starring the archetypal teen rebel James Dean, who was in fact in his mid-twenties – and *The Wild One* (1953) – starring Marlon Brando – jeans became city clothes, the urban uniform for millions of young men and part of the trinity of blue jeans, T-shirt and black leather jacket. The key words in these film titles – 'rebel' and 'wild' – hinted to the fashion world that the young, at least, no longer included within their wardrobe the suits, shirts and ties of mainstream white collar society.

The motorbike gangs on which *The Wild One* was based alarmed the public and aroused considerable media attention. It was the clothes that the gangs wore that came in for scrutiny and condemnation and, in the late 1950s, the American Institute of Men's and Boys' Wear launched its campaign to discourage the wearing of jeans in American high schools. But soon the black leather jacket and blue jeans were to part company, and

Marlon Brando raising hell in denims and a black leather biker jacket in *The Wild One* (1953).

With suits symbolizing the authority of their fathers and a pre-war attitude to conforming to society, many young men in the 1950s cast off their jackets and ties and let their shirts hang loose over their trousers. Certainly the sheer physicality of rock and roll encouraged less restrictive clothing.

while for the next 20 years the biker jacket continued to be associated with chain-wielding Hell's Angels, blue jeans were to be adopted by a much wider audience than urban kids. By the 1970s jeans were probably the most democratic items of clothing available and, with the advent of designer jeans in the 1980s, were to be raised to cult status.

## Colourful Ties and Hawaiian Shirts

In the 1950s not only youth rebelled. In their efforts to kick over the traces of the struggles of the war years, many older men recognized

that things would never again be the same and started to adopt less formal modes of dress. In an attempt to enliven the drabness of their de-mob suits and the 4 million items of khaki army surplus – everything from jumpers to jeeps – that the Americans had decided to sell off in August 1945, many men sported a range of highly decorative ties, hand-painted with scenes of exotic sunsets, pin-up girls, flowers, skyscrapers and even scenes of the American way of life. Queues formed outside Cecil Gee on London's Charing Cross Road in 1946 when it became one of the first English stores to import American ties, shirts and re-styled Zoot suits.

One of the most popular shirts to be introduced by the Americans in the 1940s was the Hawaiian shirt: even U.S. President Harry Truman (seen here) wore one.

In the 1930s men's jackets had been short, ventless 'bum freezers', fitted at the waist and hips and padded at the chest and shoulders. The wide-shouldered Zoot suit of the 1940s ushered in a new roominess and comfort that would last until the mid-1950s. Its silhouette was to be further popularized by American stars of stage, screen and sport, and was sometimes known as the Boxer Style since it was worn by the Bronx Bull, champion Jake Lamotta. Where women had Dior's 'New Look', the style for men was promoted as the 'Bold Look'. Prestigious tailors and the mass-produced garment industry supported the Zoot suit, particularly because in the 1950s the jacket seemed under threat of extinction.

Surprisingly, this threat came in the form of men's shirts. Young men were the first to cast off their jackets and leave their shirt tails hanging loose outside their trousers as suspenders (braces) became synonymous with pre-war menswear. The shirt invasion began in the late 1940s with the arrival of the Hawaiian shirt: boldly-patterned, loose-fitting and often brightly-

**Put luxury first – with underwear of 100% Acrilan.**

Vests and pants of Acrilan are soft and smooth, light and wonderfully warm.
They will never shrink, stretch, sag or felt when washed, and they dry
quickly and need no ironing. Acrilan wears superbly and can never,
never get moth in it.

Underwear by **Tenbra**

**Acrilan** is the regd trademark for the acrylic fibre supplied by **Chemstrand Ltd,** 8 Waterloo Place, London SW1

Far left: Hawaiian shirts
maintained their popularity
throughout the 1950s when they
became available in the latest
easy-care fabrics like washable
rayon.

Left: The post-war period saw a
huge number of new fibres and
fabrics introduced by chemical
companies whose wartime
materials development could now
be applied to the civilian
marketplace.

coloured, even President Truman had one. By
the end of the decade the Chat Way shirt, with
its wide open neck, three-quarter-length sleeves
and two hip-level pockets, had given birth to the
shirt-jacket. And even when jackets were still
obligatory at work and in smart circles, they were
softened by the use of half or skeleton linings

(also known as English linings). The sheer
weight of a fabric was now no longer a measure
of its quality, and menswear was introduced to a
brand new range of lightweight, ventilated
artificial and synthetic fabrics.

Ventilated fabric both insulated and air-
conditioned the body due to its open-weave mix of

merino and cross-bred wools. This fabric also had the ability to return to its original shape after it was scrunched up in the hand but, because it was expensive, it was largely confined to the luxury and custom tailoring market. In the growing ready-to-wear men's market, innovations came in the form of synthetic petrochemical fibres like Dacron (in Britain known as Terylene), Orlon and Dralon. All of these fibres, when mixed with 45 per cent wool, were lightweight, kept their shape and were wrinkle-free. The age of permanent-press pants and drip-dry no-iron shirts had arrived! Often marketed to women on these labour-saving merits, there were drawbacks for the men who wore them: the garments could be uncomfortable – a nylon shirt was cold when first put on and on a hot day felt like being trapped in your own personal sauna – and, in many cases, were badly cut. Furthermore,

these permanent-press pants did in fact need pressing at some stage but often scorched or melted under too hot an iron. Nevertheless, by 1955 artificial and synthetic fabrics had taken hold of menswear and were soon to be found in leisure clothes, underwear and, eventually, entire suits.

## Teddy Boys

The influence of America on European menswear at this time did not go unchallenged. In the early 1950s England's youth met the casual style of dress from America with their own home-grown style which consisted of the drape jacket and drainpipe trousers. London, long the centre for traditional masculine style, was where the very concept of the English gentleman had been

The American way of dressing – easy, bright and casual – did not go unchallenged. Many commentators, including tailors, saw the American style as a negative force to be countered by traditional male elegance. On London's Oxford Street in 1952, three dandies test public reactions to their assault on the 'cult of the ordinary'.

created. The Teddy Boys, however, were not of aristocratic descent but drawn from London's working-class neighbourhoods, though they appropriated a style of clothing that came from the very top of the British social classes.

Immediately after the Second World War, officers from the Guards cultivated a look that was reminiscent of the days of King Edward VII – a golden age for the style-conscious Englishman. When out of uniform these officers took to wearing long single-breasted jackets with high buttons, narrow shoulders and velvet-trimmed collars. Their narrow trousers were an off-duty version of the tight-fitting breeches worn by mounted Guards. To complete the look, the elegant man-about-town would wear a brocade waistcoat, a narrow-brimmed bowler hat (a Derby), a Chesterfield overcoat, gloves and carry a silver-headed cane or a tightly-rolled black umbrella. Until recently the uniform of the City Gent and the archetypal image of the Englishman, this ensemble was born partly out of a dislike or distrust of popular American culture in all its manifestations – youth, rock and roll, comic books, chewing gum, pronunciation of the English language and dress styles which were perceived as sloppy rather than casual. The neo-Edwardian style was also an attempt to maintain ideas about the natural order of British society, though the time of its 'ruling class' was now largely passing. The look was, not surprisingly, popular with the middle classes and the upper

classes – hence its survival amongst stockbrokers in the City of London – and was associated with dapper figures such as theatrical designer Oliver Messel and *Vogue* photographers Cecil Beaton and Norman Parkinson.

In late 1953, however, the elitist aura surrounding the Edwardian style was shattered by reports that gangs of youths from the East End of London had adopted the same look as their street

The return of the well-dressed English gentleman first came in the form of ex-Guards officers and their neo-Edwardian style tailored suits. Their rather elitist style, with its associations with a ruling class that by and large was no longer ruling, was to be appropriated by many working class British youths.

drainpipe trousers and his enormous crepe-soled shoes, known politely as 'beetle crushers' and less so as 'brothel creepers', the Ted was as interested in fashion as youth rebellion to the extent that fashion contests were organized to find The Best Dressed Ted.

While the original neo-Edwardian look was purely British, the Teds' style did, in fact, directly borrow elements from America: the Slim Jim ties, the hair cuts – either US military-styled crew cuts (called Spikey-Tops) or rock and roll DAs (where heavily greased and, for the day, outrageously long hair was swept back and over the head into a little point at the nape of the neck to resemble a duck's tail) – and even the sideburns, which can be traced back to those sported by Yankee general Ambrose Burnside during the American Civil War!

The Teddy Boys' style marked not only the ascent of British working-class youth into the sphere of fashion but also the entry of the British as a whole into the new American-style consumer society: a Ted's drape, for example, could cost between £30 and £100 (depending on whether it was off-the-peg or custom-made) at a time when the average teenage wage in Britain was around £6 a week.

## Cutting a Dash

A second assault on American cultural and fashion hegemony appeared in the mid-1950s with the emergence of Italian fashions. Three cities were to define the look for menswear: Naples, synonymous with *guapa*, a bright, flashy style of dress; Milan, which was the home of English-inspired tailors Agostino Caraceni, Baratta, Pozzi and Vuggi; and, of course, Rome, where the Academia dei Sartori trained the country's finest tailors, Brioni, Cucci, del Rosso and Giuliani, and where the international elite flew in to make a movie at Cine Citta or to shop on the Via Veneto.

The neo-Edwardian style of clothing, when worn by working-class youths, gave them their nickname: Teddy Boys. Although pertaining to be an 'English look', in fact, the Slim Jim ties, crew-cut or heavily-greased D.A hairstyle, and even the sideburns worn by some Teds were American in origin.

uniform. Between 1954 and 1956 the British press was filled with reports and comments on street muggings, vandalism and race riots carried out by these 'cosh-boys' – so called because of their favoured weapon. The media outrage and the moral panic it engendered focused on the most visible aspects of the 'cosh-boys', their neo-Edwardian style of dress, which in turn gave rise to their nickname, the 'Teddy Boys'. Instantly recognizable by his drape – a thigh-length four-button box-cut jacket with a full back (i.e. it had no central seam so that it fell better) – his

Post-war Italy was to offer a range
of menswear styles
varying from the bright Neapolitan
style to the classic tailoring of
Milan and Rome. Here, three different suits for the 'Italian
Gentleman' for the winter season,
1956/7.

There were a number of reasons for the new international desire for Italian goods when following in the tradition of *fare figura* – cutting a dash. Firstly, compared to the general shortages in the mid-1950s, Italy seemed to have an abundant supply of luxury goods, in particular, textiles. Unlike in Britain, where most were continuing to 'make do and mend' – repairing clothes and having old suits refurbished and restyled – in Italy there was little or no textile rationing. Secondly, this ready supply was accompanied by low prices for both retail and manufacturing: the weak state of Italy's labour unions at this time allowed employers to keep wages low. Finally, Italian goods had an inbuilt marketing device: they carried with them the reputation of traditional craftsmanship. Reputation alone was no guarantee of quality for overseas markets. To counter this problem, manufacturers in Biella, the capital of the Italian textile industry, linked up with leading tailors to demonstrate Italian quality and style. In 1950, a future acknowledged leader in men's suits, Nino Cerruti, took over his family's textile company that specialized in producing high-quality woollen fabrics. As a method of promoting the family name Cerruti commissioned four stage plays for which he designed the costumes. It would not be until the next decade that Cerruti would move into menswear design and manufacturing in a big way with the launch of his knitwear line in 1963 and his first men's ready-to-wear collection in 1967.

Stylish Italians of the 1950s had removed all traces of their recent fashion past – the black and brown shirts that were the uniform of fascism – to develop an image consisting of narrow trousers (without pleats and in imitation of blue jeans in the arrangement and distribution of the pocket), winkle-picker pointed shoes or loafers and the Roman Jacket which was short enough for the wearer to be seated on a Vespa or Lambretta motor scooter without the jacket hem touching the seat.

Italian fashions were to have an international impact as the industry reorganized itself to cater for a growing ready-to-wear market. Each year, manufacturers organized increasing numbers of trade shows and more and more Britons and Americans returned home after their Roman holidays. For American men the Continental Look became a serious rival to the Ivy League look with its standard grey flannel 'Number One Sack Suit', as it was known at Brooks Brothers. Meanwhile, in London, clothier Cecil Gee, who had kicked off the new decade by importing American clothes, was by the end of the 1950s stocking his new store on Shaftesbury Avenue with Italian fashions. Stylish youths in search of the latest Italian shirts and shoes were flocking to John Stephen's shop in a Soho backstreet that would soon become the fashion headquarters of the Swinging Sixties: Carnaby Street.

The latest in jacket styles – the Nehru collar – demonstrates its ability to turn heads at the San Remo International Festival of Fashion in 1963.

# Sharp Suits and Bell-Bottoms

If Savile Row was the temple of classic elegance, then in the 1960s Carnaby Street was a national institution – and tourist attraction – which symbolized the new attitudes in male dress that would be referred to as the 'Peacock Revolution'.

Between 1962 and 1965 Carnaby Street became a focal point for the Mods. This group took their name, a derivative of 'modernist', from their passion for modern jazz music as performed by Dave Brubeck and Charlie Mingus as opposed to the more traditional New Orleans jazz that was popular at the time. The Mods also idolized rhythm and blues and soul singers James Brown, Ike and Tina Turner, Aretha Franklin and The Temptations, but the Mods' true passion was fashion, and their lives revolved around shopping, buying and wearing clothes. Rejecting the now dated fashions of the Teddy Boys, they took their cue from the sophisticated lines of Italian and French fashions.

In opposition to the Mods were the Rockers, who maintained biker jacket, motor cycle and rock and roll music. The Rockers'

style seemed completely archaic to the Mods, who, when they were not wearing parkas for riding their Vespas or Lambretta scooters, cultivated a 'clean' image exemplified by polo shirts, turtleneck sweaters, immaculate – preferably white – trousers or clean jeans, Clark's suede Desert boots and double-vented, three-button jackets with narrow lapels and flap pockets. Mods' heads were equally well dressed: hair was cut and carefully lacquered into the 'Perry Como' or 'French Crew' cuts. The ultimate in style for the Mod male was a 'two-tone' mohair suit.

Although their origins have been traced back to around 1958, the Mods achieved public notoriety in the spring and summer of 1964 when, for several months running, the beaches around Brighton were the scene of violent clashes between Mods and Rockers. These clashes were sensationalized and to a large extent inflamed by reports in the British tabloid press.

The first half of the 1960s saw the Mods in ascendance. The nationwide music television programme *Ready, Steady, Go!*, which

Above: Carnaby Street, London, home of the swinging sixties boutiques that dressed the Peacock Revolutionaries.

Left: Mods and Motorscooters: a clean-cut style of dress and hair did not make them all 'nice boys'. Through the summer of 1964 Mods and Rockers violently clashed on the beaches of Brighton.

Above: While Mods went for modern jazz and R&B, and French or Italian fashions, their arch rivals the Rockers maintained the biker jacket, motorbikes and rock and roll music from America.

Opposite: Mod accessories: note the 'no-tie tie' with elastic neckband and the checked spats. By the 1960s young men were starting to be recognized by manufacturers and advertisers as a lucrative and as yet untapped market.

Opposite below: John Stephen's Carnaby Street His Clothes, the flagship store in a chain that made him the 'Mod Millionaire'.

began broadcasting at 6.06pm on Fridays in August 1963, was a showcase for Mod fashions, music and their dances – the Locomotion, the Hitchhiker and the Dog – while the clubs the Mods frequented – The Scene, Ad Lib and the Marquee Club – were the home of bands like the Animals, the Kinks, the Yardbirds, Manfred Mann and, above all, The Who (whose 1965 hit 'My Generation' could be seen as the song of times) who would be part of the 'British Sound' that would dominate pop music throughout the 1960s.

## Retail Revolution

Retailers answered the demand for the new and the modern by offering affordable clothing for the young that was also exciting to shop for and to wear. While the more affluent Mod could afford to have the European styles of suits and shirts copied for them by numerous East End tailors, most searched out new additions to their wardrobes at mass outfitters like Burtons and John Collier or at new boutiques such as John Michael on the King's Road and John Stephen's shop His Clothes on Carnaby Street.

In 1958 John Stephen became the first clothier to open a shop on Carnaby Street. His

Clothes was the flagship store of a chain of boutiques: by 1961 Stephen had four shops, by 1964, six and by the following year he had expanded beyond Soho with a further ten Lord John shops in London and two in the seaside town of Brighton. The press dubbed Stephen, at the age of 28, the 'King of Carnaby Street' and the 'Mod Millionaire'. Stephen's rise to fame was due to his understanding of the likes and dislikes of the new youth market whose interests in popular music and club culture were, to a large extent, recreated inside his boutiques with

piped music and spotlights. Furthermore, the sales staff were young and fashionable and encouraged customers to try on the garments that were displayed on rails and racks rather than behind counters.

Such retailing devices were revolutionary and broke with the traditional stuffy – even church-like – atmosphere of menswear departments and outfitters. Another lasting effect of his approach to fashion was his advocating of stylish effects and gimmicks that were by their very nature transient, rather than the traditional attitude of 'buying for investment' or for a 'last a lifetime' wardrobe. Stephen recognized that his customers wanted new clothes and wanted them often.

## Beatlemania

In the 1960s the influence of American music and fashion was largely in decline. As in America around 1959, rock and roll music was being linked to delinquency and by 1962, in Britain, rock and roll went 'underground' in the face of the emerging mass-appeal 'pop'. The shift in emphasis and style can be seen in the clothing of the leading 'Mersey sound' band of the decade. In 1961, the Beatles still dressed in the style of rock rebel Gene Vincent: black T-shirts and black leather biker jackets. A year later and with the influence of new manager Brian Epstein, the future Fab Four swapped their rebel outfits for sharp suits, crisp, white shirts with rounded collars, neckties and tie pins. By 1963 Beatlemania was sweeping the country and their style guaranteed sales of the low-necked, collarless jackets that had been designed by Pierre Cardin in 1960. The Beatles' version of the 'Beatle jacket' was, in fact, made by tailor-to-

The Beatles in the low-necked collarless jackets that had originally been designed in 1960 by Pierre Cardin. The Fab Four's version of the Cardin jacket was made by tailor to the stars, Dougie Millings. The look is completed by Beatle boots with a pointed toe and stacked heel.

the-stars, Dougie Millings. Also popular were 'Beatle boots' or Chelsea boots with a pointed toe and high heel which were low-cut with elastic side vamps.

## The Return of the Dandy?

When the Beatles conquered America the world's press suddenly became interested in and aware of British fashions. Many declared that the Dandy had returned because of the increased amounts of colour that were now being seen in menswear. This observation, although true about increased colour, was erroneous regarding the Dandy: Beau Brummel, the original eighteenth-century Dandy was, in fact, opposed to lots of colour in menswear and was the man who believed that waistcoats could be decorative but suits must be plain. However, 1960s retailers such as John Stephen and Rupert Lycett Green, the owner of menswear outlet Blades, had endured the drabness and darkness – both physical and psychological – of the Second World War and felt the need for brighter men's clothing. At Blades, suits designed by Eric Joy were coloured white, pink, cream, mustard as well as grey, black and blue. Lycett Green stated that the well-dressed modern man should own two dinner jackets, one velvet evening suit, one grey suit, one black suit, two 'working' suits, a lightweight tweed suit for the country, two lightweight summer suits and a 'crush-proof' suit for travelling! He also needed at least three overcoats in winter, two sports jackets, six pairs of slacks and around 50 shirts.

One of the first to sport coloured clothes was the designer David Mlinaric of Tite Street, who favoured cinnamon-coloured suits and yellow shirts. Mlinaric went further in revolutionizing menswear when he attached

frills to the front of an evening shirt, a style that was soon copied by, among others, fashion photographer Patrick Lichfield. In an interview with the *Observer* newspaper, Lichfield admitted to owning 26 suits and argued that:

'A man should enjoy his clothes. A man doesn't dress for himself. He dresses to attract the girls . . . all men dress to be sexy like cock pheasants in the mating season'.

As such personalities publicly proclaimed a man's rights to the delights of fashion, the interest in menswear sparked a debate over definitions of handsomeness as more and more young men (and some not so young) abandoned the traditional identifying codes of masculinity in favour of 'effeminate' colours and longer hair.

## Boys will be Girls

The forerunners of this 'Peacock Revolution' were a handful of shops in the West Soho backstreets that included Bill Green's store Vince, situated close to Marshall Street swimming pool, a popular haunt for London's homosexual community. Green, a former photographer for men's 'muscle' magazines, made a name for himself in the fashion industry by selling by mail order skin-tight jeans and clinging black sweaters that he had seen worn in France in the 1950s. Green's shop also drew a wide clientele from the arts and music for his brightly-coloured shirts, pink jeans and low-waisted trousers, the 'hipsters' or 'hiphuggers'. John Stephen had been a sales assistant at Vince before opening his own shop and it was often jokingly pointed out that Stephen's boutique His Clothes should have been called Her Clothes!

A dark grey DB city suit with front vents and slim trousers from the 1966 collection of the Group of Five, a new generation of French tailors who aimed to create 'haute couture' for men.

Champions of the new trend in 'effeminate' clothing were the Rolling Stones but the trend was also to be felt in Paris where the Group of Five aimed to create *haute couture* for men. Founded in 1956, the Five – Andre Bardot, Jose Camps, Socrate, Gaston Waltener and Max Evzeline – were a new generation of tailors who presented their collections to the fashion press twice a year until 1968. While they were applauded for their attempts to liven up menswear with their embroidered vests and modern textiles, they were

Mick Jagger, lead singer with The Rolling Stones and champion of the Peacock Revolution trend in 'effeminate' dress for men. The sleeves, cuffs and laced front of Jagger's shirt are reminiscent of the flamboyant men's fashions of the eighteenth century.

unanimously condemned for their encouragement of men to carry handbags, even if they did call them 'man cases'.

Eventually, and despite the efforts of Jose Camps to reduce the cost and the number of fittings on a customer from three to two by basing each customer's suit on standardized patterns – one per size – in a sort of semi-custom-made tailoring, the Group of Five faced a shrinking clientele and their styles were to falter in the face of the new wave of ready-to-wear lines from Pierre Cardin.

## Pierre Cardin and the French Line

The 1960s saw a revolution in the production and distribution of menswear following a pattern similar to the women's ready-to-wear industry. From now on, menswear would, like womenswear, be focused on either a 'label' or a designer name with new collections presented each year.

Pioneering a new system in licensing agreements between designers and ready-to-wear manufacturers was Pierre Cardin. Born in Italy in 1922, Cardin served his apprenticeship

French *couturier* Pierre Cardin's first men's ready-to-wear collection from 1960 owed a debt to 'classic' English menswear, featuring tweeds and worsteds. The mid-calf 'Space Boots' mark the collection as Cardin and of the 1960s.

as a tailor and had worked briefly for the *couturiers* Paquin and Schiaparelli before joining the newly-founded house of Dior in 1947. Three years later Cardin started his own company, initially specializing in film and theatre costumes: Cardin had made the magnificent costumes for Jean Cocteau's *Beauty and the Beast* (1947). In 1953 Cardin presented his first *haute couture* collection of womenswear and opened his first shop, Eve, which was joined in 1957 by – naturally enough – Adam, a boutique of clothing and accessories for men. Two years later, Cardin was banished from the Couture-Creation list of the Fédération Française de la Couture for daring to present a collection of women's *prêt-à-porter* (ready-to-wear) garments. He was to be swiftly reinstated after his example was widely copied by other *couturiers* who had realized that the shrinking number of clients who were sufficiently wealthy to buy *couture* was not enough to keep their businesses afloat.

In 1960 Cardin extended the designer label ready-to-wear strategy to menswear and launched his first collection at the Hotel Crillon in Paris. The style, sometimes known as the 'Youth line' or the 'Cylinder line', owed a great deal, in fact, to the existing 'English style' with its close-fitting silhouette: jackets were narrow-shouldered and fitted at the waist and had high sleeveholes while trousers were high-waisted and flat-fronted i.e. with no pleats. Instead of hiring the usual actors and professional models to show his clothes, Cardin employed students, a measure that was in itself enough to rouse the interest of the press. What the assembled commentators saw were the small, collarless and tail-less jackets – in corduroy for winter and striped cotton for summer – that the Beatles would make famous the world over.

Cardin's 'Sports' collection for winter 1973-74. Cardin's continued financial success is due to his astute business acumen. Under licensing agreements, his name is associated not only with fashion clothing but with accessories, perfumes and even canned foods and baby buggies.

Following the success of the show, the next year Brill, the garment manufacturer, brought out the first complete line of men's ready-to-wear clothing signed by Pierre Cardin and, for the first time, ready-made suits had a recognizable 'line' and a recognized designer name attached to them. But although they were ready-to-wear, Cardin's suits were still out of the reach of most men's pockets and it would be another three years before his financial success was assured. By 1965 it was estimated that more than half a million men were wearing Cardin's clothing and further licensing agreements followed, in particular in

England, where he signed deals with
Associated Tailors who had a chain of 400
stores. Under licensing agreements designers
give manufacturers permission to use their
name and/or designs for which they are paid a
percentage of sales. The most obvious example
of a licensing agreement is one between a
designer and a chemical company who produce
designer perfumes. Licences allow designers to
diversify and now cover nearly every imaginable
product. Pierre Cardin is the most financially
successful with nearly 400 licences which include
men's and womenswear, children's wear, hats,
shoes, hosiery, jewellery, sunglasses and scents,
even furniture, canned fish, scuba diving suits
and, most recently, the designer baby buggy!
Licensing agreements are geographical: a Pierre
Cardin suit purchased in America will have been
manufactured under licence in the United States.
Nevertheless, all designs are undertaken in
Cardin's studio and his agents control the
quality at the various licensed manufacturing
houses around the world.

Menswear labels spawned in the wake of the
Cardin licensing example include Ted Lapidus
(who dressed the Beatles and also supplied
their short-lived Apple boutique), Lanvin,
Christian Dior, Pierre Balmain, Hubert de
Givenchy, Guy Laroche and Louis Feraud.
Some had been tailors but most, before their
venture into men's ready-to-wear, had started
their careers as *couturiers* of womenswear.
Combined, these designers helped to make
Paris the capital of men's luxury ready-to-wear
and encouraged the next generation of
designers like Nino Cerruti and Yves Saint
Laurent to set up shop in the city.

## California Cool

From small beginnings in Haight-Ashbury in
San Francisco, by 1965 the California hippie

Left: In the 1960s many designers,
such as Yves Saint Laurent, who
had made their names as *couturiers*
of women's clothing ventured into
the menswear market.

movement began to overtake 'Swinging
London'. The movement was a culmination of
factors: psychedelic, mind-expanding drugs;
student political activities inspired by the Civil
Rights movement of Martin Luther King and
the Anti-Vietnam War demonstrations and a
latent west-coast beatnik tradition of non-
conformism. The new generation of drop-outs,
who refused to join the system and rejected the
consumer society, instead sought self-
knowledge through the use of hallucinogenic
drugs, Eastern mysticism and attempts at
communal, self-sufficient living.

Spreading the gospel of this alternative
philosophy were rock personalities – Jefferson
Airplane, Grateful Dead, The Doors and Jimi
Hendrix – and the rock festivals at which they
appeared – Monterey in 1966, Woodstock in
1969 – became the new gathering points for
youth. Even the Beatles came under the
influence: in 1967 the Fab Four left for India
and enlightenment in the form of their own
personal guru, Marharishi Mahesh Yogi. When

Far left: Louis Feraud established
a House in Cannes in 1949 which
was patronised by the film stars
who made the annual pilgrimage
to the film festival. In 1960 Feraud
moved to Paris and began his
ready-to-wear business.

they returned, the Pierre Cardin-inspired sharp suits were gone and were replaced by caftans, Afghan coats, sandals and cheesecloth shirts.

The hippies' disdain for consumer society and all its manifestations led to their rejection of a fashion system of built-in obsolescence. Despite the democratization of fashion by the ready-to-wear industry, new clothes were rejected in favour of second-hand and old clothes that were patched and embellished with embroidery.

By 1966 the Mod movement in London had largely died out and the retailers on Carnaby Street cashed in on the new hippie look by filling their stores with cheap cottons, incense, and Indian music. New boutiques opened: in Portobello 'I Was Lord Kitchener's Valet' revived Edwardian splendour by selling second-hand regimental uniforms like the ones on the cover of the Beatles 1967 *Sergeant Pepper's Lonely Hearts Club Band* album. On the King's Road the reference to the hippie drug culture was evident in the name of 'Granny Takes a Trip'. But the most sophisticated London hippie men's fashion shop was 'Mr Fish' owned by Michael Fish who began his career on Jermyn Street – famous for its traditional men's shirts and outfitters – before moving in 1962 to Turnbull and Asser where Fish launched the appropriately named wide 'Kipper tie' that would by 1965 make the narrow Mod ties a thing of the past. In 1966 Fish opened his own store at Clifford Street – at the bottom of Savile Row – which was to become the place where the 'beautiful people' – the rock stars, celebrities

Far left: Flamboyant 'Peacock' Jimi Hendrix. Hendrix's ensemble demonstrates the various cultures which influenced menswear in the 1960s: Afghan-style jacket, velvet trousers and American Indian-style buckskin boots.

Centre: Portobello boutique I was Lord Kitchener's Valet sold second-hand regimental uniforms made fashionable by The Beatles who wore them on the cover of *Sergeant Pepper's Lonely Hearts Club Band* album in 1967.

Left: The sophisticated hippie courtesy of Mr Fish on Clifford Street, London, the place where the 'beautiful people' and celebrity hippies shopped.

and even the occasional titled hippie like Lord Lichfield and the Duke of Bedford – bought their clothes in order to 'express themselves'. While the hippie style may have passed, the legacy of 'being yourself' and dressing to 'express' the 'real you' have nevertheless remained and from the 1970s onwards have come to inform new directions in menswear.

# Fashion and Anti-Fashion

While men's fashions in the first half of the century were largely dictated by the elite of society, in the post-Second World War period, the youth revolution, mass production and mass consumption exerted their influences on the 'rules' of dress. The 'trickle-down' theory, developed by Thorsten Veblen in 1899 and refined by Georg Simmel in the early part of this century, which holds that fashion is launched at the top of the social structure and eventually works its way down to the bottom, was challenged by fashions that were no longer concerned with merely symbolizing class or its aspirations, but rather with the expression of sexual, political, ethnic and even religious identities.

Contemporary menswear was henceforward to be marked by pluralism, a proliferation of styles, some from fashion designers but many coming up from the street which were then adapted and mixed together by various groups or 'style tribes'.

The unstable economic conditions and the political and social unrest of the late 1960s – assassinations, riots, civil disorder – were to

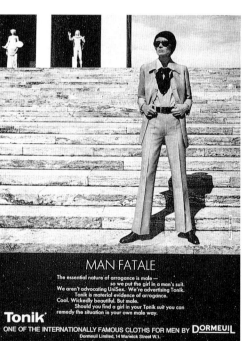

MAN FATALE

The essential nature of arrogance is male —
so we put the girl in a man's suit.
We aren't advocating UniSex. We're advertising Tonik.
Tonik is material evidence of arrogance.
Cool. Wickedly beautiful. But male.
Should you find a girl in your Tonik suit you can
remedy the situation in your own male way.

**Tonik**
ONE OF THE INTERNATIONALLY FAMOUS CLOTHS FOR MEN BY **DORMEUIL**
Dormeuil Limited, 14 Warwick Street W.1.

continue in the following decade as awareness of the growing inequalities in society grew. Gay Liberation, Women's Liberation and ecological and peace movements which focused concern on the environment, pollution, the extinction of wildlife species, nuclear power and nuclear arms proliferation, alongside militant trade union

*Right: 'Unisex' styles were popularized in the 1960s by designers such as Ted Lapidus, who gave the decade the Safari jacket. As more men took to wearing floral patterns and soft flowing-sleeved shirts, women were increasingly adopting men's garments, and the decade saw the arrival of trousers suits for women.*

*Far right: One of the earliest fashion trends of the 1970s was to wear old clothes, a trend which caused the British Clothing Manufacturers Federation to protest that 3 out of every 10 British men were the worst dressed in Europe.*

activities, were to change the face of society. No longer were class and gender the defining social divisions: race, ethnicity, employment and unemployment, youth and age, would all be reflected in the multitude of fashions and styles in menswear.

## Second-hand Style and Retro-dressing

By 1970 there were 1 million unemployed in Britain and by 1979 the number would grow to over 3 million. The effects of the first oil crisis in 1973, when OPEC raised their prices, had a knock-on effect as workers were laid off and the prices of manufactured goods rose. One of the earliest fashion crazes of the decade was to wear old clothes, a trend which caused the British Clothing Manufacturers Federation to protest in 1975 that 3 out of every 10 British men were the worst dressed in Europe. While army surplus clothing was functional and hence popular, the 'new poor' of the unemployed needed new clothes on a budget. With youth unemployment also rising, second-hand clothing and army surplus was given fashion cachet as specialist shops opened selling only old clothes. Ironically, as the influence of fashion kicked in, prices of second-hand clothes went up dramatically, often taking them out of reach of the very people who needed them most. Popular treasures were 'granddad' shirts: collarless, over-sized and with long U-shaped tails that were worn loose outside waistbands. Such items helped to fuel the appeal for 'retro-dressing', one of the most important trends in fashion in the early to mid-1970s. Unsurprisingly in the depressed economic climate it was the 1930s and 1940s – years of making do and mend – that were revived. *Bonnie and Clyde* (1967) and *The Great Gatsby* (1974) not only helped to popularize the fashions of the

Stark contrasts in style in the 1970s but both look to the past for their inspiration: above, the anti-materialism of the patched look owed a debt to 1940s' 'make do and mend' attitudes, while the 1930s provided the styling influence for Ralph Lauren, costumier for the *The Great Gatsby.*

1930s to a new generation, who searched through the second-hand shops for genuine Burberry raincoats, silk shirts, Harris Tweed jackets and double-breasted pinstriped suits; they also encouraged designers to revive the classics. Furthermore, *The Great Gatsby* launched its costume designer, Ralph Lauren, into the international limelight. Born in the Bronx in 1938, Lauren's success lay in his timely recognition of the traditions and values of the past – and the myths associated with that past. Like most designers, Lauren looked to the past – real and fictional – for inspiration, altering details to suit the present, but he was one of the first designers to translate recent historical dress into successful marketing concepts with products based on mythical American male archetypes such as the hunter, the cowboy, the countryman and the man-about-town.

A second style, also inspired by 1930s fashion but far removed from the WASP wardrobes created by Lauren, was the pimp look, best expressed in the movie *Super Fly* in which black pimps 'pimp-roll'-walked the streets of Harlem to an Isaac Hayes soundtrack, dressed in flamboyant, pagoda-shouldered jackets with piped or velvet-edged lapels, flared trousers with high-pointed waistbands and fancy belt loops and large soft hats.

## Designer Denims

Surprisingly, the pair of jeans had undergone few fashion variations since its origin as workwear in the nineteenth century. Levi-Strauss, Lee and Wrangler saw increased profits as more and more young men – and women – turned to jeans as leisurewear, but it was not until the 1970s that manufacturers were able to turn jeans into a fashion commodity subject to stylistic change.

Denim sales were to reach their zenith in the 1970s. According to the International Institute for Cotton, in 1970 in Britain alone sales

Denim jacket, polka dot tie, creaseless trousers and scuffed suede shoes: this is the 1970s' style in menswear condemned by the British Clothing Manufacturers' Federation.

for the more colourful of the species

**VANDERBILT FOR MEN BY MURJANI**
Designer Jeans for men now available at selected branches of Burtons

Not a designer, more a famous name to add status. Gloria Vanderbilt licensed her name to jeans manufacturers Murjani and joined the 'designer denims' wars, doing battle with Calvin Klein, Giorgio Armani and *Dynasty* star Joan Collins.

amounted to 12 million pairs, worth around £26 million. By 1976 this had increased to 38 million pairs worth £243 million while worldwide sales of jeans reached 170 million pairs worth around $13 billion, with Levi-Strauss the biggest clothing manufacturer in the world. Increased sales were largely due to the popularity of flared trouser styles in the 1970s which gave jeans manufacturers the opportunity to produce styles to suit a wide range of customers, now including the middle-aged and middle-class white collar workers who began to wear jeans as leisurewear: even President Jimmy Carter was wearing denims! And as high-income

earners dressed down in denim, the fashion industry responded to the new market and designer jeans were born.

Calvin Klein was the first to market 'exclusive' – even though they were mass-produced – 'signature' jeans. In 1978 Klein launched a jeans line cut to suit the particular proportions of the new 'middle market': 'Re-fitted and Well Cut Calvin's' that suited the young at heart but the wide in girth who snapped up 200,000 pairs in the first week, even though they cost 50 per cent more than a pair of Levi's. By 1980, more than 30 designers including Marithe and François Girbaud, Joseph and Armani were joined by signatures from Gloria Vanderbilt, Joan Collins and even the famous New York discotheque, Studio 54' in becoming associated with designer jeans for men and women.

Left: By the 1970s even U.S. President Jimmy Carter wore jeans as standard leisurewear.

Above: Denim's official sanction occurred when it appeared on the catwalks of Paris and Milan with ready-to-wear designers like Versace, Armani, Joseph, Jean-Paul Gaultier and Katharine Hamnett offering 'signature' jeans.

## All That Glisters . . .

If the essence of hippie living in the 1960s was a belief in the natural and the authentic, the Glam Rock and Glitter Rock styles of the 1970s epitomized artificiality and parodied the notions of fashionable dressing in a sartorial flamboyance of rhinestones, sequins and satins. The leading exponents of the style were musicians and

look was referenced again in the huge padded shoulders of jackets, clashing colours and the use of deliberately shiny, glittery and slinky artificial fabrics like rayon and nylon.

The theatricality of the Glam and Glitter styles meant their most acute manifestations were confined to the stage, discotheques and

performers: David Bowie's incarnations as Ziggy Stardust and Aladdin Sane, Gary Glitter, Alvin Stardust, Roxy Music and the New York Dolls tottered precariously on 1940s-inspired but grossly over-height silver, gold and multi-coloured platform shoes and boots. The 1940s

clubs. Glam rock fans and glitter dressers largely divided into two camps: teenyboppers who followed the mainstream glitter bands like Gary Glitter, Marc Bolan and Alvin Stardust, and other, older fans who followed the more esoteric artists like Bowie, Roxy Music and Lou Reed.

Nevertheless, because they had appropriated earlier styles into their own fashions, both streams shared the same 'retro' tendencies found in other 1970s fashions: to create myths about the past to inspire in the wearer a sense of glamour and nostalgia.

The Glam and Glitter Rock of the 1970s extolled artificiality, parodied all notions of accepted good taste and in some cases, blurred even further the traditional gender distinctions in dress. David Bowie (above, left) would initially epitomize the more esoteric side of Glam compared to mainstream artists like Gary Glitter.

Taking a walk on the wild side with
Lou Reed.

The Return of the Dandy? New
Romantics Adam and the Ants
'retro dressing' as eighteenth-
century highwaymen and
swash-buckling pirates.

## No Future?

Running counter to the sequinned elegance of the glam rock performers, whose lyrics, dress and reported lifestyles were far removed from everyday life in the 1970s, was Punk, the counter-cultural movement which claimed to speak for the neglected working-class youth of a Britain that was lurching from one economic crisis to another. The post-war prosperity that had sustained the expansive mood of the 1960s in Europe and America had now disappeared to be replaced by a downward spiral of economic inflation and industrial recession.

Punk shared Glam Rock's assault on notions of good taste, but appeared to be a style dedicated not to glamour but to ugliness and alluded to sado-masochism in its 'bondage trousers', studded dog collars and chain belts. The name Punk was itself appropriate: the term had always been associated with cheapness and physical and moral rottenness and had in the sixteenth century even been associated with prostitution.

Punks took garments that were recognized symbols of the establishment: business suits were slashed and stuck with safety pins, and ties were worn with slashed T-shirts. Jeans, the archetypal clothing of the hippie generation and, then, the ultimate symbol of a designer-led consumer society, were 'attacked' and 'vandalized' with rips. Accessories were constructed out of the detritus of the material world from which these young urban dispossessed were alienated: razor blades, safety pins, garbage bags and even rats.

Punk style seems to have emerged in late 1974, around the time that Malcolm McLaren – who had formed and was now promoting the punk rock band The Sex Pistols – renamed the shop he co-owned with Vivienne Westwood on the King's Road. In 1971 the shop had started life as Let It Rock, one of the last bastions of Teddy Boy style. In 1972 it became Too Fast to Live, Too Young to Die, but in 1974 was renamed simply Sex (and would change again in 1977 to Seditionaries), for which Westwood designed bondage trousers and clothes inspired by corsetry and fetish wear in leather and rubber.

The power to shock, however, is always short-lived: by 1976, The Sex Pistols had achieved not only notoriety with 'Anarchy in the UK' and their version of 'God Save the Queen' but had spawned a whole range of alternative, anti-establishment and underground styles that were largely related to the increasingly fragmented music scene.

The post-Punk years from 1977 to 1978 saw the rise of Ska-inspired Mods in anonymous dark suits and pork pie hats. Even more anonymous were the fans of Joy Division who sported military uniforms at the band's concerts. Meanwhile techno-futurists like Devo with their signature tune 'We Are Not Men, We Are Devo' and the German band Kraftwerk with their track 'Man Machine' inspired a post-holocaust style of dressing in boiler-suits, decontamination outfits and survival suits. In 1978 McLaren opened 'PX' as a sort of 'techno-bunker' lit by neon, displaying leather jump-suits hanging on metal netting. The equivalent boutique in Paris was Survival, an atomic bomb shelter to the north of the Les Halles district where discerning survivalists and last action heroes could buy dyed black uniforms, gas masks and survival rations.

Always adept at reading the signs of the times, in 1979 Malcolm McLaren transformed PX into a New Romantics boutique like World's End on the King's Road – another McLaren-Westwood exercise in exploiting the segmented youth market.

The New Romantics responded to global crises by retro-dressing as swash-buckling pirates and eighteenth-century highwaymen in outfits largely supplied by theatrical costumiers. Their make-up, frilled shirts, gold braid-trimmed jackets and skirts – even if they were really Scottish kilts as

sported by Gary Kemp, the lead singer of New Romantic band Spandau Ballet or the re-styled caftans as worn by Culture Club's Boy George – were nevertheless an onslaught against one of the most fundamental divisions in modern society: gender. Gay or straight, 'Blitz Culture' – named after the club where the New Romantic fashions began – allowed men to experience transvestism – to 'masquerade' as women, to do some 'gender bending'. Most importantly, however, the New Romantics' attitudes to male dress marked an increased interest in menswear that in the 1980s would encourage designers to add men's lines to their seasonal womenswear collections.

Above left: Not a cowboy hat in sight: Punks in Dallas, Texas in 1984.

Above right: Johnny Rotten. A recognized symbol of the establishment – the blazer jacket synonymous with schools, sports teams and gentlemen's clubs – under attack from the safety pin.

Left: Gender bending with Boy George of Culture Club.

Top: Manufacturers like Adidas responded to the developing leisure industries of the 1970s with new ranges of sportswear, active wear and leisure wear.

Below: By the end of the 1970s, *Esquire* estimated that there were 30 million joggers in America.

## Functional Fashion

While, on the whole, less money was spent on clothes in the 1970s, by contrast the amount spent on leisure – sports and holidays – was rising. This was perhaps due in part to the changing working patterns faced by many. While workers who had spent years doing a job they thought they had for life faced redundancy, some of the luckier jobless received redundancy pay-outs which went some way in helping to 'structure' their leisure time. Others who held on to their jobs faced the prospect of becoming one of the increasing numbers of part-time workers. It is not surprising that the 1970s saw the rise of new industries devoted to leisure and that the garment industry

responded with sportswear. Sportswear was more than just a wardrobe of leisure clothing: it implied a break with the tradition of wearing the 'Sunday best' suit and came to refer to a whole lifestyle, epitomized by the running shoe and the fleecy, hooded jogging suit. By the end of the decade *Esquire* estimated that there were around 30 million joggers in America, including one Jimmy Carter.

The functionalism of sportswear began to make inroads into the working wardrobe. Collars and ties gave way to jersey polo shirts and T-shirts; suit jackets began to lose their nipped-in waists and little by little became transformed into the blouson-style casual jacket. Jeans loosened up as 'baggy thigh' versions became popular and the tight-fitting, bell-bottom flared trousers of the early 1970s were replaced by peg-top styles – full at the waist but narrow at the ankle – in a sort of city version of the jogging pants.

One of the leaders in luxury men's leisurewear and sportswear in the 1970s was Daniel Hechter, who founded the Men's Fashion Designer Club in France in 1978 with other sportswear designers – most notably, Jean Cacharel, Faconnable and Marithe et Francois Girbaud. The club organized widely-publicized fashion shows to promote men's clothing that was more versatile than the traditional garments being presented by the suit designers and bespoke tailors. What marked the club's collections was a new silhouette created by soft, 'unstructured' clothes. The aim of these garments was to make suits and jackets lighter and more comfortable and resulted in unfitted jackets with loose armholes and rounded shoulders, lower buttons, longer lapels and shorter tails. By the end of the decade the 'unstructured' silhouette dominated menswear and came to be associated with one designer in particular: Giorgio Armani. It was a silhouette that would persist until the mid-1980s when the business suit was re-born with the young, upwardly mobile professionals who turned to 'Power Dressing'.

# Dressed for Success

The 1980s will be remembered as the designer decade, one where men were no longer merely customers, but truly fashion consumers. In 1975, men's ready-to-wear accounted for just under 8 per cent of the *couturiers'* direct profits; by 1985, the figure had gone up to nearly 20 per cent. Where made-to-order did survive, for example, in the bespoke tailoring of Savile Row, it had largely lost its ability to dominate taste. It was ready-to-wear that would come to embody the spirit of fashion.

The decade witnessed a sustained effort on the part of designers and advertisers to capture the lucrative male market. The new male fashion consumer was catered for by the advent of men's fashion and lifestyle magazines like *Cosmo Man*, *GQ*, *The Face*, *i-D* and *Arena*. The Condé Nast publishing empire extended its range to include *Vogue Men*, *Uomo Vogue*, *Vogue Hommes* and *Vogue Hommes International*, a semi-annual fashion supplement to match the monthly issues. While the editorial of the magazines concentrated on the clothes, the advertising

# Calvin Klein Underwear

So desirable was the brand name on the elastic waistband of Calvin Klein underwear, a fashion developed for displaying it by rolling over the waistband of jeans.

was increasingly to demonstrate the interest of the new male consumer in grooming aids – beauty products for skin and hair, aftershaves and colognes and accessories – everything from underwear, watches and cars to computers, beers and exercise.

The international fashion calendar now included the spring and autumn showings at SEHM (European Menswear Show) in Paris, Pitti Uomo in Florence, the Scandinavian Menswear Fair in Copenhagen, International Men's Fashion Week in Cologne, and IMBEX

(International Men's and Boys' Wear
Exhibition) in London as well as major shows
in New York, Tokyo and Milan. Further
interest in menswear was provided by
television and the movies: John Travolta in
*Urban Cowboy* (1980) kicked the decade off
with a 'modern western' look; after *Top Gun*
(1986) came a craze for flight jackets.
Harrison Ford gave us the worn leather
bomber jacket after he sported one in *Raiders
of the Lost Ark* (1981) while 1987 signalled a
return in interest in the suit and tailoring
following the wardrobe designed by Giorgio
Armani for *The Untouchables* (1987). If *Miami
Vice* influenced casual dress for several years –
finely-groomed designer stubble and T-shirts
worn under unstructured jackets – then
Michael Douglas' striped shirt with white
collars and cuffs – known as the 'gekko' shirt
after his character Gordon Gekko in the movie
*Wall Street* (1988), became the sartorial
symbol of the yuppie traders on the world's
stock exchanges.

When the movie and rock stars were not
on stage or on screen they were busy
endorsing designers. A highly competitive
market meant designers went to great lengths
to ensure the audiences at their showings were
liberally sprinkled with celebrities: Elton John
at Gianni Versace, Eric Clapton at Giorgio
Armani while actor John Hurt and more
recently Alexander McQueen, head designer at
the house of Givenchy, have both stepped
onto the catwalks as models for Comme des
Garçons.

In the 1980s nearly all the fashion labels
produced a men's line: Thierry Mugler (1980);
Claude Montana (1981); Kenzo, Byblos and
Comme des Garçons (1983); Jean Paul
Gaultier (1984) all diversified into menswear.
By 1986 John Galliano, Jean Muir, Wendy
Dagworthy, Franco Moschino and Katharine
Hamnett added their collections to the

growing number of menswear lines. The
'Napoleon of Couture', Karl Lagerfeld, head of
the house of Chanel, acknowledged market
forces and joined their ranks in 1989.

Michael Douglas as Gordon
Gekko in *Wall Street* (1988). The
'Gekko shirt' – striped with plain
white collar and cuffs – became
the shirt of yuppie 'movers and
shakers' in the financial markets.

The world's money markets and stock exchange fuelled the consumer credit boom of the 1980s while television shows like *Miami Vice* showed men how to spend their money: designer suits, t-shirts, carefully-groomed designer stubble and, of course, a Ferrari.

## The Retail Revolution

The early 1980s saw a renewed interest in shops
and their design. In 1982 Terence Conran and
George Davies salvaged the remains of British
menswear chain Hepworths, recasting it as the
trendsetting store Next. The interiors – exposed,
polished wood, glass, chrome and well-positioned
cut flowers in glass bowls – were designed by
David Davies Associates and gave retail shop
design the kick start it needed. Regrettably, the
style would be indiscriminately applied to a whole
range of retailers until it became little more than a
cliché. Hot on the heels of Next came Next Too,
Next Essentials and Next Accessories: between
1983 and 1987, Davies was to launch menswear,
womenswear, footwear, accessories, cosmetics,

Above: With top of the range
designer ready-to-wear out of most
people's league, designers realized
the potential of the brand name
and launched bridge collections.
In addition to the ready-to-wear
with *couture* prices of Giorgio
Armani, are Le Collezione and
Emporio Armani, retailed in a new
generation of designer boutiques.

Left: The 'enfant terrible' of
fashion, Jean-Paul Gaultier tried –
and failed – to put men in skirts.
However, the ensuing press
attention ensured publicity for
Gaultier's menswear and bridge
collection, Junior Gaultier.

lingerie and, to complete the entire lifestyle for the 1980s' consumer, home furnishings, florists and cafes. And, there was also the *Next Directory*, a glossy, Filofax-inspired mail-order catalogue.

Another retail leader is Moroccan-born Joseph Ettedgui. By the time he opened his flagship store on Sloane Street in London (designed by no less an architect than Sir Norman Foster, architect of the Hong Kong and Shanghai Bank building) there were already ten Joseph shops in London. The cool, high-tech interior of the building made Joseph one of the front runners in fashion retailing: restaurants (Joe's cafes) and lifestyle (Joseph Pour la Maison) were to follow. For Ettedgui, fashion was as much to do with where you went and how you organized your life as with the clothes you wore.

Following in the footsteps of the fashion chains came a new generation of designer boutiques: Kenzo, designed by Eva Jiricna (who also designed the Joseph interiors); Katharine Hamnett at Brompton Cross, London (designed by Norman Foster) and in Glasgow (by Nigel Coates); Jean Paul Gaultier (designed by Ron Arad who also had his own shop selling interiors and furniture ideas) and Issey Miyake (by Armstrong Chipperfield in black slate, Portland stone and white marble to produce a ' modern Zen' interior) were some of the most visually arresting and the places in which to be seen shopping. From New York to Tokyo, the pattern was repeated.

The suit strikes back at Dior.

## The Suit Strikes Back

In the 1980s, Britain, the United States and Germany all saw a swing back to the political right. Instead of Jimmy Carter's casual denims, the new Reagan administration favoured suits and military uniforms. President Reagan rebuked the military men who had not been wearing their uniforms in Washington and from 1 May 1981, the US Navy ordered all its officers and men back into full uniform. The same year, US Secretary of State General Haig was voted the best dressed man by the Custom Tailors' Guild of America. In England, the Menswear Association of Britain nominated the former 1960s swinger and dedicated follower of fashion, Patrick, Earl of Lichfield as their choice. No longer the dandy, Lichfield adopted the conventional look with hand-made suits.

Along with the suit came the waistcoat which advertised the wearer as a man who could afford a three-piece suit: in the early 1980s a bespoke, Savile Row three-piece suit would cost around £800; a two-piece would cost around £300. For those on an even tighter budget, help was at hand from ready-to-wear designer suits from Monsieur Dior at around £150.

The suit's climb back up the fashion ranks began in the late 1970s in Italy when the textile industries centred around Prato (near Florence), Como and Biella (to the north and west of Milan respectively) began to produce cloths that were specially designed for ready-to-wear suits. As well as being much cheaper – cloth with a virgin wool content of over 50 per cent was gradually abandoned in favour of producing low-cost cloths from waste wool – these fabrics accommodated the fashion industry whereby new collections, new ideas, new colours and new patterns are presented each season. 'Made in Italy' now meant an alliance between textile companies and the designers, the former becoming the ready-to-wear manufacturers of the garments conceived by the designers.

Engineering this system was Giorgio Armani. Armani presented his first ready-to-wear men's line in 1975, manufactured by Turin textile giant Gft who also make parts of Valentino Uomo ready-to-wear. Over the seasons Armani increasingly cut away at the structure of suits by removing padding and interlinings, a very useful tactic for mass manufacturing as all the parts that really give a suit its shape are dispensed with. The unstructured stylishness of Armani's suits in 1980 are best demonstrated by the clothes he designed for Richard Gere in *American Gigolo*, and his double-breasted suits as worn by Don Johnson on and off the set of *Miami Vice* became the indispensable sign of the well-dressed man. The height of shapelessness came in 1985 when Armani presented men's suits in unstructured linen, recalling the humid atmosphere of Havana in the 1930s and 1940s.

Crumpled chic was to be challenged by the return of the business suit, a return that coincided with a general financial euphoria which gave rise to the junk bond kings and high-powered investment brokers in the money markets of the world. Men got down to business in suits from Armani, Hugo Boss – as worn by the scheming wheeler dealers in television's *Dynasty* – Nino Cerutti (who dressed a wicked Jack Nicholson in *The Witches of Eastwick*) or Ralph Lauren.

The way a man looked was so important that image consultants began to appear, advising politicians and captains of industry on how they should dress to impress. The idea caught on in the mass market as major department stores started to employ consultants to assist men in their wardrobe selection. There were even manuals for the purpose, like Lois Fenton's *Dress for Excellence* that gave tips on how every man could dress like a 'Master of the Universe'.

'Excellence' and 'elegance' were the buzz words of the late 1980s and they were

Above: Ronald Reagan's
administration favoured suits and
military uniforms: on 1 May 1981,
the U.S. Navy ordered all officers
and men back into full uniform.

Right: Giorgio Armani's
re-invention of the suit. Since his
first collection of men's ready-to-
wear in 1975, Armani steadily cut
away at the structure of the suit,
removing paddings and
interlinings to create an
unstructured stylishness. The
result was a suit that could be
mass produced yet still carried
the cachet of the designer name.

accompanied by a renewed interest in the 'classics' of menswear. Footwear companies benefited as the classic styles from Church's Fine English Shoes, Trickers, Cole Haan, Bass and Dexters enjoyed a new popularity. Burberrys and Barbours came out of the country closet as city wear and companies who had no connection with fashion began to trade on their 'heritage' by launching ranges of men's accessories: Alfred Dunhill of tobacco fame provided cufflinks, 'small leathers' (belts, gloves and wallets) and even polo shirts to co-ordinate with cigar cutters and cigarette lighters, and Ferrari and Porsche were on hand to provide designer sunglasses.

## What's In a Name?

In 1896 Gaston Louis Vuitton put his initials LV on his luggage to distinguish it from imitations. In 1933 Rene Lacoste marketed his 'alligator' tennis shirts that he had been wearing on the courts since 1927. In the 1960s Pierre Cardin cashed in by putting his signature on his neckties and then went on to apply his name to tuna fish and scuba outfits! By the 1980s, names, logos and initials were the weapons in an all-out war between designers and manufacturers competing for business. Everything from shirts, jackets and trousers to ties, belts, socks and underwear carried initials (Christian Dior's CD, Yves Saint Laurent's YSL, Calvin Klein's CK) or a logo (Lacoste's alligators, Fred Perry's laurel leaves, J.C. Penney's fox, Pringle's lion, Ralph Lauren's polo player, Henry Cotton's fisherman and even Hugh Hefner's Bunny Club bunny) it was becoming harder to find a simple T-shirt that did not have a logo, initial or slogan on it. Even labels – which used to be stitched discretely into the inside neckband – were now on full view, over-sized and on the front. So coveted were designer labels that a host of urban myths of gang warfare arose: youths killing each other for their Eight Ball jackets and high-top

Reeboks, and schoolyard bullying of kids who did not have the latest gear. Bodies became the new site for advertising with labels like Chipie, Naf Naf, Chevignon, Soviet, Diesel, Avirex and Creeks emblazoned across chests, backs and bottoms. Even the soles of shoes became advertising venues for the logos of Nike, Reebok and Adidas. As the fashion for slogans spread worldwide the craze assumed surreal qualities when Japanese teenagers wore T-shirts and jackets decorated with meaningless phrases like 'Go School Turkey Fish'.

Copies of designer merchandise, from *haute couture* to accessories, became widespread: sunglasses that looked just like Ray-Bans, watches that (at a distance) could pass for a Rolex or a Cartier and aftershaves that were bottled and packaged just like Chanel, Dior and Armani. This battle was not so much between individual designers for customers but between the 'real' and the 'fake' designer labels.

What's in a name?: The Lacoste alligator and Church's shoes.

Left: Companies with little or no
connection with clothing also
began to trade on their names and
history. Alfred Dunhill of tobacco
fame offer not only cigarettes and
lighters but a whole range of high
quality accessories for the well-
dressed man.

Above: Walter de Virlis, the
founder of Soviet.

## Dressing Down

Caught in the wake of the financial crash of 1987 were the fashion companies and retailers who suddenly experienced huge downturns in sales. The sombre mood of the economic recession of the late 1980s was exacerbated by a whole range of other social and political issues: AIDS, the break-up of the Soviet Union, the rise of ethnic nationalism in Yugoslavia, famine in Africa and global warming to name just a few. The general sobriety was matched in fashion, particularly by the Japanese designers who had come to international attention in the early years of the decade. The confused state of the world and of the individual within it was reflected in designs from Comme des Garçons which concealed the body and did away with conventional European structures in clothing, while Yohji Yamamoto offered trousers that seemed too short and jackets with sleeves that seemed too long, combining to create an out of kilter look that was in keeping with the spirit of the times.

While these Japanese styles were never directly translated to the street, they nevertheless reinforced two key features of late 1980s men's fashions: the vogue for all things black and the continuation of the shapeless silhouette established by Armani at the beginning of the decade.

The sombre mood following the financial crash of 1987 was reflected in men's fashions. Yohji Yamamoto reinforced two key features of men's fashions in the late 1980s: the vogue for black and the continuation of the unstructured 'shapeless' silhouette begun by Armani at the beginning of the decade.

# Action Men and Global Warriors

Despite the recession and the consumer credit squeeze of the 1990s men continued to buy fashionable clothing and fashion-related goods. The fashion industry's success in a period dominated by economic, social and political troubles was largely due to its acknowledgment that its market had radically altered in composition since the 1980s and its subsequent development of niche marketing techniques.

In 1989, *Vogue* reported that the 30 plus age group was increasing and predicted that, by the end of the century, there would be one million fewer 16 to 24 year olds in Britain alone. By the 1990s, the fashion industry was taking note of financially secure older couples who found themselves with increased disposable income now that their dependent children had left home. The problem was that these 'empty nesters' were not necessarily spending their money on fashion, not surprising since the industry since the 1960s had largely been geared towards the taste of the youth market.

Although the mass of the mass market was still out there, it now consisted of numerous fractured groups, each with their own identity.

Designers and their advertising agents played on these different identities, often devising themed collections which allowed customers to slip in and out of each identity at will.

The numerous fractured identities of the Post Modern Man are evidenced by the wide variety of fashion looks available today.

## Homo Po-Mo

Commentators on the 'post-modern condition' have argued that, over the past century, we have witnessed the gradual erosion of secure collective identities, leading to the increasing fragmentation of our personal identities. The traditional forms of reference by which we and our place in society can be defined – social class, occupation, income, religion, nation – are in decline as a result of the increasingly rapid and widespread rate of social change. For example, economic globalization – the trend, seen in the fashion industry itself, for investment, production, marketing and distribution to take place on an international basis rather than in a single country – contributes to the erosion of traditional sources of identity, with a resulting overlapping of those identities. In the fashion industry, under these conditions, it is now possible to have a French-born designer, working in Britain, showing collections in New York of garments made in the Philippines in a factory owned by a Hong Kong-based consortium.

Few viable forms have emerged to take the place of these lost sources of identity. In our post-modern age, it is images created by the mass media and popular culture – television, cinema, music and, of course, fashion – that provide us with references – albeit unstable ones – to construct our collective selves and personal identities.

What we buy and what determines what we buy is increasingly influenced by images from television and advertising which, for their part, refer to popular culture. The surface appearance of things has become of paramount importance: the way fashion looks predominates at the expense of substance or meaning. Like pop music, fashion quotes, tastes, samples and mixes elements to create new sub-cultural and pan-cultural identities.

The suit according to Comme des Garçons.

## Desperately Seeking Something

The identity crises of the 1990s prompted the fashion industry to differentiate male markets in terms of lifestyles. These concepts were reinforced by advertising and developments in fashion retailing. The 'New Man', as he was referred to by the media, could be one of any of a type which included 'sophisticated man' (intellectual, socially aware and cosmopolitan), 'discontented man' (unhappy with his current identity and seeking to change it), 'pleasure-seeking man' (macho and hedonistic), 'achiever man' (status-conscious and ambitious), 'action man' (thrill-seeking, adventurer), 'conventional man' (traditionalist and conservative) and 'aesthetic man' (sensitive, caring and artistic).

Each New Man needed the right clothes to express his media-created identity. He could now choose from three kinds of apparel groups: non-fashion basics, fashion basics and high fashion. Many department stores began to cater to the range of New Men by establishing physically different sales areas, each with suitably evocative names such as 'The Sportsman' and 'Man About Town'. In addition, Ralph Lauren's in-store Polo boutiques, for example, employed the same visual identity that was used in the free-standing Polo shops: dark woods enhance a wardrobe built around the often mythical and media-invented traditions, values and legends of a historic American way of life – the America of Hemingway and rugged pioneering individuals. Thus, Lauren potentially could capture any, or even all, of the New Man types and provide him with a suitable wardrobe.

By the mid-1990s, two further kinds of new men were identified: the 'New Lad' and 'Iron

The suit according to Savile Row.

John'. New Lad indulged in a hedonistic lifestyle while Iron John was more like a traditional chauvinist. According to *Elle* in 1992, New Man, New Lad and Iron John were distinguishable by their clothing: Iron John wore practical, casual, non-designer clothes with boxer shorts for underwear. New Lad was easily spotted in the wild in Versace, Montana and Calvin Klein. Close examination revealed New Lad to prefer Y-fronts. New Man, however, went for Romeo Gigli, The Gap, Agnès B and Nicole Fahri over the top of his Paul Smith boxer briefs.

## The Real Thing?

One of the dominant tendencies in fashion has been the post-modern pastiche, the eclectic mix of historical styles and influences. The search for 'authenticity' and the 'original' is one of the main counters to this. Yet precisely because the most attractive authentic clothes often belong to a culture other than our own, they take on different meanings as they cross class, race, gender and cultural divides. Take, for example, the Barbour jacket – the green, waxed, hunting-shooting-fishing garment synonymous with the outdoor life. These jackets have recently been appropriated as the height of urban chic by Italian football fans. On the streets of London, Barbour wearers signal the authenticity of their jackets by keeping the gilt badge on the collar lapel. Thus, in efforts to create an identity for ourselves, we turn to that of someone else, even if it has been created by designers, advertisers and stylists.

In the early 1990s, West Indian 'Rude Boys' imitated the rapper M.C. Hammer by wearing baggy Pascalou jeans – often two or three sizes too big – made by Chipie, while in the United States some young men were wearing their clothes inside out in imitation of rappers Kriss Kross. Others, following the group Jodeci, adopted the 'Prison Look' in honour of the young men who went straight from the ghetto to the penitentiary. Jodeci's shaven heads were covered by hats made up of sleeves cut from sweatshirts and knotted at one end. Soon, however, the look was picked up by manufacturers and designers like Calvin Klein. Now every young, white, middle-class French, British or German youth could share the same identity.

Men's fashions have become a growth industry. While the clothes remain more conservative than womenswear, still based largely

on shirts, jackets, trousers and suits, there is a greater variety in cut, colour and fabric which, in turn, has reduced the cycle of men's fashion to the seasonal collections. The Paris menswear collections in January 1997 showed the ability of the current generation of designers to acknowledge traditional tailoring and to present street style through the popular culture of today. Paul Smith showed high-buttoned Regency-style jackets and velour suits alongside PVC snakeskin suits and raincoats; Yohji Yamamoto displayed his 'no frills' trademark: pure lines and

Above: Action Man (thrill-seeking, outdoor type) meets Conventional Man (traditional and conservative) in clothing provided by Barbour.

Left: The New Man, courtesy of Calvin Klein: caring, sharing, thoughtful and no longer 'Obsessed'!

Above: Fashion for the 1990s:
oversized baggy trousers.

Right: 1997 Paris menswear
collections: Yohji Yamamoto's
leather trench coat.

Noten turned back the clock with soft-shouldered wool jackets teamed with Oxford Bags. While each designer acknowledged the tradition of tailoring, past styles and even ancient religions (Yamamoto's 'Modern Zen'), Jean Paul Gaultier sent shaven-headed models down the catwalk to the sounds of Ska music in 1990s' versions of 1970s' Skinhead clothes: bovver boots, braces, tartans and Prince of Wales Check.

These new developments in menswear have coincided with a rise in the number of men's boutiques which are once again challenging the near monopoly of gentlemen's outfitters, department and chain stores as suppliers of fashions for men. And not only are collections of menswear more widely available, but men themselves have entered the predominately female model industry to the extent that some are approaching the fame of their supermodel sisters. So visible are they in the fashion world today that male models have even been used to promote womenswear: Matthew, Nathan, James Neal and Jamie Spear from Select successfully enticed the teenage shopper and her mother into French womenswear retailer Kookai.

interesting fabrics in six shades of black in a military-inspired collection of fatigue trousers and floor-sweeping leather trench coats. Veronique Nichanian for Hermes gave achiever man something to aim for with a collection in cashmere, alpaca and silk-crepe while Dries Van

1997 Paris menswear collections.
Top left: Hermes chic in alpaca
and cashmere. Below left: Jean
Paul Gaultier's Bovver Boys.
Above: Paul Smith mixes Regency
styles and PVC.

## Extreme Sports, Extreme Fashions

One of the major developments in menswear over the past decade has been the increased number of garments and styles in the fashion wardrobe that have their origins in sporting clothes. For some, such sporting incursions offered fashionable touches, but for others, the development of fashion sports clothes has led to the creation and maintenance of complete looks.

The fitness craze of the 1970s first encouraged the sales of sports clothing and shoes, but their wear, by and large, remained confined to sporting activities. In the following decade, many started to appreciate the functional nature of sports apparel, and jogging suits, muscle shirts and training shoes began to be worn as leisurewear. Soon, designers got in on the act, and by the 1990s, Chanel was offering designer running shoes complete with the back-to-back Cs of the Chanel logo, Paul Smith gave us designer mountain bike and road cycling gear, and Calvin Klein and Donna Karan transformed the humble jogging suit into fluorescent, fleecy street clothes. Spandex cycle shorts, worn by bicycle couriers who had 'stolen' them from Tour de France riders, had their padded crotches ripped out and were worn as club wear. Tennis heart-throb Andre Agassi began a craze for wearing cycle shorts under tennis shorts, presumably because his legs chaffed. Soon it was the thing to wear two pairs of different shorts for any sporting activity: rugby, soccer and jogging to the corner shop.

The sports of the late 1990s are extreme sports: off-road, off-piste, whitewater, white-knuckle speed freak sports are for the new 'real men'. The sportswear market is one of the fastest growing sectors in the fashion industry and one where advances in fibre and fabric technology are increasingly appropriated by ready-to-wear designers for both their novelty value and their production of identity-kit clothing.

Where authentic sports clothing today can improve performance and, thanks to a host of new reflective and thermal conductive fabrics, even save your life, designer versions at least let you look as though you know the difference between rap-jumping, zorbing and boardercrossing.

A whole new market is growing up and some are quicker to respond to its potential than others. In the autumn of 1996, original and designer versions of the firesuits worn by Indy Car racers Michael Andretti and Christian Fittipaldi, both by Donna Karan, went on sale in the United States. Ralph Lauren now offers 'Polo Sport' aftershave and body splash while Paco Rabanne has put his new fragrance for men – called, of course, 'Paco Rabanne Man'– in vending machines placed conveniently in the men's locker rooms of gyms. In the mean time, 'authentic' sports clothes and accessories companies like Serious, Avirex, Adidas, Puma, Berghaus, Bolle, Oakley, Swobo and O'Neill continue to dominate the active sports clothing market and exert an increasing influence on the designers of ready-to-wear menswear.

Right: Leading players in active sports clothing and accessories, like Oakley, are finding that specialist clothing for extreme sports is making the crossover into fashion both at street level and on the catwalks.

The influence of sportswear on the street and, above, on the catwalk at Versace.

## Fashioning the Future

Recent trends in men's fashion have demonstrated the extent to which fashion has become a feature of everyday life and one that is no longer confined to, or determined by, the elite in our society or even by the top designers. The styles of the future cannot be accurately predicted though we know that future fashions will be influenced by a number of traditional contributing factors.

The economic, social and political climate in which we will live, the new roles we will adopt in society and the continued influence of the mass media and popular culture will all contribute to the shape of fashion in the future.

Equally formative will be our own attitudes to fashion and taste, but, increasingly, desire for new styles every season may well be tempered by a heightened awareness of ethical and ecological issues surrounding the production of the raw materials of fashion and their manufacture.

Many industries are adapting to both consumer pressure and government legislation in these areas, but the fashion industry is a constant paradox: it thrives on its own obsolescence. The short lifecycle of fashion is what maintains consumption, and often the comfort, function and even pleasure of wearing clothes is neglected in favour of novelty.

Nevertheless, there have been recent attempts by designers and manufacturers to address ecological issues: for some, this address has been forced upon them by legislation, for others, it is out of genuine concern. Patagonia, makers of 'outdoor' clothing for walkers, skiers, snowboarders and the like, donate 1 per cent of all sales to environmental causes. Arvind, the world's largest exporter of denim, was the first denim mill worldwide to be certified by the 'Eco-tex' Consortium in Germany for fulfilling the criteria for ecologically optimized fabrics.

For many companies, 'green issues' remain a

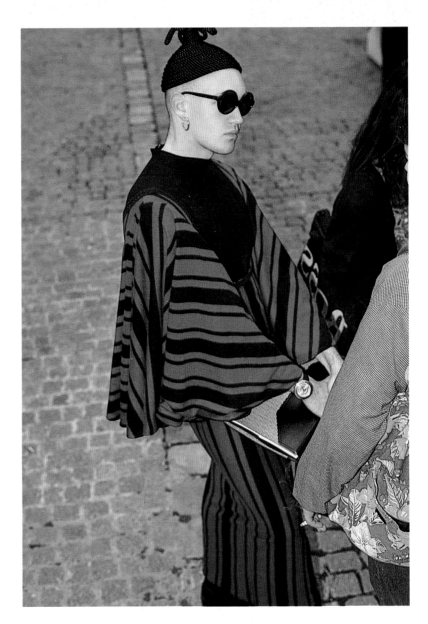

The Sweet Smell of Success:
Calvin Klein's CK1 unisex scent.

one

Calvin Klein

*a new fragrance for a man or a woman*

cynical marketing strategy, though one of the
effects has been the campaign against the fur
trade. Not only furs but also tortoiseshell, ivory,
certain birds's feathers, reptile skins of
endangered species and even badger and boar
hair (used for the manufacture of quality hair
and shaving brushes) have disappeared or are in
the process of disappearing from fashion.

Natural fibres – wool, cotton, linen and silk –
which may seem a logical alternative to the
chemical processes of the synthetic textile
industry have been shown to be equally
problematic. Because production of natural
fibres is largely confined to developing nations,
and pesticides and organo-phosphates (some of
which are banned in the West) are required in
large quantities for their successful cultivation,
fibres such as cotton may not be as 'green' as
they first appear. Furthermore, their production
raises ethical issues regarding the exploitation of
labour and the demise of traditional and local
industries. Cheap labour, low manufacturing
costs and lax environmental controls have
encouraged multi-national corporations to set up
shop in developing countries rather than at
home where increasingly tough new laws on the
discharge of pollutants and 'polluter pays' (for
clean-ups of illegal and accidental waste
disposal) policies are in force.

Yet as economies shift, so to do relations
between the 'First' and the 'Third' World. The
'sweat-shop' manufacturers of South East Asia –
traditional areas of cheap labour that produce
many of the fashion goods bought in Western
shops – are disappearing as their countries'
economies grow stronger. These countries may
well begin to rival the West in both economic
and design terms. Like the rise of Japanese
designers in the second half of the twentieth
century, the fashion world can look forward to
the time when fashion innovations come from
designers from Malaysia, Korea and Taiwan who
will swell the ranks of the current generation of
new designers from non-traditional fashion-

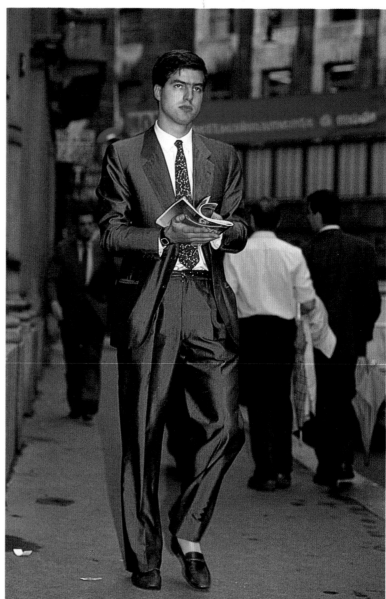

producing sources such as The Netherlands, Belgium and Scandinavia.

A recent success of the fashion industry has been the acknowledgement of consumers' willingness to recycle: we have all at one time or another, either through circumstances or through choice, worn second-hand clothing, maybe as 'hand-me-downs or from one of the growing number of 'designer second-hand' clothes stores. We are also more open to the concept of recycling because we have experienced it in a whole range of other areas, for example in the packaging of cosmetics from pioneers The Body Shop. Likewise many fashion garments already include quantities of recycled materials.

Tencel is a regenerated fibre produced by dissolving wood pulp – itself a waste product of the paper-making industry – in amine oxide, a chemical commonly found in shampoo. These fibres are considerably stronger than cotton and when Tencel fabrics are printed with reactive dyes, they require no polluting caustic treatment. Called the 'newest high-tech natural' fibre, Tencel is now a popular choice with jeans manufacturers: Calvin Klein, Guess?, Gap, Levi's Silvertabs and Doc Marten Apparel are all using Burlington Denims, (the third largest producer of denim fabric in America) Tencel-injected denim; meanwhile Swift Denim have produced Soda Pop Denim, a blend of cotton and Fortrel Ecospun: six plastic soda pop bottles find their way into each pair of jeans and not into a landfill site.

Fibre technology could reduce the number of clothes we wear. When garments made from Rhovyl Thermovyl chlorofibre, Montedison's Meraklon or Du Pont's Thermax are worn next to the skin, the skin is kept warm and dry by a wicking action, transferring any cooling body moisture into a more absorbent outerwear garment. Alternatively, 'artificial intelligence fibres' developed by Teijin, Toray and Kanebo,

amongst others, automatically adjust a garment's colour from black to white, and vice versa, according to temperature, making the wearer psychologically and thence physiologically 'feel' warmer. And inorganic carbon particles added to fibres can warm the body of the wearer by converting near infra-red radiation from sunlight into thermal energy.

If the number of garments we will be wearing in the future shrinks, so too might their size. As our planet becomes more crowded, living spaces become smaller. The ultimate in 'space-saving' clothes would be those made from Elastane or Spandex fabrics which stretch up to 500 per cent before breaking but also have a high rate of recovery – they return to their original shape after stretching.

Because life is tough on the streets, how about clothing made from Kevlar? Developed by Du Pont, Kevlar has been used in 'ballistic protective jackets' (as they are officially known). Woven from coarse aramid (high-strength fibre) yarns, many layers are 'superimposed' as a composite fabric that is able to resist most low and medium-energy bullets and shrapnel. Also available – fortunately – in simpler forms where 'less protection' is required, Kevlar is still cut, puncture and abrasion-resistant. Furthermore, Kevlar clothes are flame-resistant and self-extinguishing.

Whatever the future holds, one thing we can be sure of is that men's interest in fashion has been realized by designers, retailers and, above all, by themselves. Whether it's a made-to-measure suit from the finest of Savile Row tailors, designer-ready-to-wear, chain store basics or do-it-yourself mix-n-match, there will be something in the future guaranteed to suit.

## Further Reading

Bennet-England, Rodney, *Dress Optional*, Peter Owen, 1967

Brush Kidwell, C. and Steele, V., *Men and Women: Dressing the Part*, Smithsonian Institution Press, 1989

Byrde, P., *The Male Image*, B.T Batsford Ltd, 1979

Chapman, R. and Rutherford J. (eds.), *Male Order*, Lawrence and Wishart, 1989

Chibnall, S., *Whistle and Zoot*, History Workshop Journal, Autumn 1985

De Marly, D., *Fashion For Men*, B.T. Batsford Ltd, 1985

Martin, R. and Koda, H., *Jocks and Nerds*, Rizzoli, 1989

Peacock, John, *Men's Fashion*, Thames and Hudson, 1996

Polhemus, T., *Streetstyle*, Thames and Hudson, 1994

Walker, R., *The Savile Row Story*, Multimedia Books, 1988

Wilson, E. and Taylor, L., *Through the Looking Glass*, BBC Books, 1989

## Picture Credits

3 Hulton Getty Collection; 4 Rex Features; 7 (top) BT Batsford Archive; 7 (bottom) Corbis-Bettmann; 8 Country Life; 9 National Portrait Gallery; 10 (left) Fashion Research Centre, Bath; 10 (right) Hulton Getty Collection; 11 (right) Hulton Getty Collection; 13 Advertising Archive; 14 BT Batsford Archive; 15 Hulton Getty Collection; 16 Hulton Getty Collection; 17 Corbis-Bettmann; 18 National Portrait Gallery; 19 National Portrait Gallery; 21 Hulton Getty Collection; 22 Advertising Archive; 23 Advertising Archive; 24 (top) Hulton Getty Collection; 24 (bottom) Hulton Getty Collection; 25 Corbis-Bettmann; 26 Corbis-Bettmann; 27 National Portrait Gallery; 28 (top) Hulton Getty Collection; 28 (bottom) Advertising Archive; 29 Hulton Getty Collection; 30 National Portrait Gallery; 31 Corbis-Bettmann; 33 (top) Hulton-Getty Collection; 33 (bottom) National Portrait Gallery; 34 National Portrait Gallery; 35 Corbis-Bettmann; 36 Corbis-Bettmann; 37 Corbis-Bettmann; 38 Hulton Getty Collection; 40 Royal and Ancient Golf Club, St Andrews, Fife; 41 Lacoste; 42 Hulton Getty Collection; 43 Hulton Getty Collection; 45 (top) BT Batsford Archive; 45 (bottom) Hulton Getty Collection; 46 Hulton Getty Collection; 48 Advertising Archive; 49 (left) Corbis-Bettmann; 49 (right) Hulton Getty Collection; 50 Hulton Getty Collection; 51 Popperfoto; 52 Corbis-Bettmann; 58 Corbis-Bettmann; 60 Advertising Archive; 61 Advertising Archive; 62 Advertising Archive; 64 Hulton Getty Collection; 65 Hulton Getty Collection; 66 Hulton Getty Collection; 68 Hulton Getty Collection; 69 Corbis-Bettmann; 70 Corbis-Bettmann; 72 (left) Hulton Getty Collection; 69 Corbis-Bettmann; 70 Corbis-Bettmann; 72 (left) Hulton Getty Collection; 72 (right) Hulton Getty Collection; 73 Corbis-Bettmann; 74 Corbis-Bettmann; 74-5 Corbis-Bettmann; 76 Hulton Getty Collection; 77 Advertising Archive; 79 Fashion Research Centre, Bath; 80 Corbis-Bettmann; 81 Corbis-Bettmann; 82-3 Corbis-Bettmann; 84 Corbis-Bettmann; 85 Corbis-Bettmann; 86 Advertising Archive; 87 Advertising Archive; 88 Hulton Getty Collection; 89 (left) Hulton Getty Collection; 89 (right) Hulton Getty Collection; 90 Hulton Getty Collection; 91 Hulton Getty Collection; 93 Hulton Getty Collection; 95 (top) Rex Features; 95 (bottom) Hulton Getty Collection; 96 Hulton Getty Collection; 97 (top) Hulton Getty Collection; 97 (bottom) Rex Features; 98 Corbis-Bettmann; 100 Hulton Getty Collection; 101 Corbis-Bettmann; 102 Hulton Getty Collection; 103 Hulton Getty Collection; 104 Hulton Getty Collection; 105 Syndication International; 106 (left) Rex Features; 106 (right) Rex Features; 107 Syndication International; 108 Advertising Archive; 109 Syndication International; 110 (top) Rex Features; 110 (bottom) Rex Features; 111 Syndication International; 112 Advertising Archive; 113 (left) Rex Features; 113 (right) Niall McInerney; 114 London Features International; 115 Corbis-Bettmann; 116 Rex Features; 117 Rex Features; 119 (left) Corbis-Bettmann; 119 (top right) Rex Features; 119 (bottom right) Corbis-Bettmann; 120 (top) Advertising Archive; 120 (bottom) Rex Features; 121 Niall McInerney; 122 Advertising Archive; 123 BT Batsford Archive; 124 (top) Hulton Getty Collection; 124 (bottom) Rex Features; 125 (top) Niall McInerney; 125 (bottom) Niall McInerney; 126 Rex Features; 128 Rex Features; 129 Niall McInerney; 130 Lacoste; 131 Advertising Archive; 132 Advertising Archive; 133 Syndication International; 135 Niall McInerney; 136 Niall McInerney; 137 (top) Niall McInerney; 137 (bottom) Niall McInerney; 137 Niall McInerney; 138 (top) Niall McInerney; 138 (bottom) Rex Features; 139 Niall McInerney; 140 Niall McInerney; 141 Syndication International; 142 Advertising Archive; 143 Syndication International; 144 (top) Syndication International; 144 (bottom) Niall McInerney; 145 (top) Niall McInerney; 145 (bottom) Niall McInerney; 145 Niall McInerney; 147 Oakley; 148 (top left) Rex Features; 148 (top right) Niall McInerney; 148 (bottom right) Niall McInerney; 148 (bottom left) Niall McInerney; 149 (top) Niall McInerney; 149 (bottom) Niall McInerney; 150 Advertising Archive; 152 Niall McInerney; 153 Niall McInerney; 155 Niall McInerney; 160 Rex Features

# Index